HIPPIE BOY

HIPPIE BOY

A Girl's Story

. . .

a memoir

Ingrid Ricks

BERKLEY BOOKS, NEW YORK

THE BERKLEY PUBLISHING GROUP
Published by the Penguin Group
Penguin Group (USA) LLC
375 Hudson Street, New York, New York 10014

USA • Canada • UK • Ireland • Australia • New Zealand • India • South Africa • China

penguin.com

A Penguin Random House Company

Berkley trade paperback ISBN: 978-0-425-27400-2

An application to register this book for cataloging has been submitted to the Library of Congress.

PUBLISHING HISTORY
Berkley eBook edition / August 2013
Berkley trade paperback edition / January 2014

PRINTED IN THE UNITED STATES OF AMERICA

10 9 8 7 6 5 4 3 2 1

Cover photo: Girl © Cheryl Casey / Shutterstock.
Cover design by Diana Kolsky.
Interior text design by Tiffany Estreicher.

For Connie—

Who was there then, and continues to be now, even from three thousand miles away.

1

. . .

December 1979

I should have slammed the door in Earl's face.

It's what I wanted to do the minute I saw him standing on our porch, snow clinging to his greasy black hair like dandruff.

He was thick and short, five feet seven at most, with pasty white skin and a bulging gut that pressed against his plaid shirt and hung in a lump over his giant silver belt buckle.

I noticed that his fingernails were stained and filled with dirt, a dead giveaway that he worked as a mechanic even if Mom hadn't mentioned it. But it was his eyes that bothered me most. They were icy-blue and hard, magnified by thick glasses that made them look like they were going to pop out of his head.

"Is your mom here?" he asked.

I stared at him, wondering what she could possibly see in him.

"Yeah, she's here," I said finally, reluctantly stepping out of the way so he could come inside.

By now my sisters, Connie and Heidi, had ventured in to check out Mom's date and I saw the same disgust in their eyes. My brothers, barely eight and two, were too young to care and stayed hidden in the playroom.

As soon as Earl entered, a smell that reminded me of rotting hamburger meat filled the air. Mom appeared a minute later. She was dressed in her standard date attire: a bell-shaped white skirt that hit her mid-calf and a ruffled polyester blouse covered in a tiny purple floral print. Her wildflower Avon perfume trailed behind her, competing with the odor coming from Earl.

Connie and I both shot her imploring looks, but she ignored us and headed straight for Earl.

"Okay, children, I'll be back later," she said. Then the two of them were gone.

In the six months since her divorce from Dad, Mom had dated her share of losers. Connie and I figured it was a phase she was going through until she got back into the swing of things. But Earl was an all-time low. He was a homeless Vietnam vet who lived in the back of his Chinook mini camper. From the bits and pieces we could gather from Mom, we knew he had been married at least twice before and had three or four kids from his previous wives. Mom told us he was a Mormon, but said he wasn't an elder. This meant that he didn't hold the Melchizedek Priesthood—the priesthood that enabled men to go on a Mormon mission and get married in the Mormon temple, and gave them the power to bestow the gift of the Holy Ghost, heal the sick, and spiritually preside over their families. In order to be ordained as an elder, a Mormon man had to be at least eighteen years of age and deemed worthy by his bishop and the stake president, the immediate priesthood leader of the bishop.

Then there was his smell. Mom said it was because he ate mostly meat, a habit he'd picked up while serving in Vietnam.

"Don't worry. There's no way she's going to marry him. He's not even a good Mormon," Connie assured me, even after Mom ignored our initial demands that she stop dating him. Connie was fifteen and the oldest, and she was so confident in her prediction that she had me convinced.

A month later, the day after my birthday, Mom called us all into the kitchen for an announcement.

"Earl asked me to marry him," she declared with a smile. "I said yes."

I was stunned. Just two weeks before, on Christmas Day, she had told us she was through with him. We'd all been gathered around our plastic, fold-out kitchen table, savoring our Christmas lunch of sloppy joes, potato chips, and raspberry Jell-O—a meal I looked forward to all year—when Mom had made the surprise announcement. She'd realized that Earl wasn't right for her and was going to tell him it was over. My sisters and I had all cheered at the news. I was so relieved I'd almost hugged her. Now she was doing a complete flip-flop, and acting like it was perfectly normal.

"But I thought you said you weren't going to date him anymore," I stammered. I could feel the panic building inside me and though I wasn't sure why, I was scared.

"Why?" Connie added. "You know we don't like him, and you hardly even know him!"

Mom shot us an exasperated look. "He's going to be my husband, and I want you to treat him with respect."

"But, Mom, he's not even a good church member." I was desperate to change her mind. It just didn't seem possible that she could actually want to marry that creep.

Mom's face turned flush. "Whatever he did in tee past is in tee past," she said in her thick Austrian accent that made all of her *th* sounds come out as *t* or *d* sounds. "He's a good church member now. He's been ordained an elder, and he's going to be my husband.

"Don't worry," she added, looking directly at me. "He's not going to try to take the place of your dad."

Of course he wasn't going to replace Dad. The fact that she'd even mentioned *Dad* in conjunction with that smelly, disgusting excuse for a human made my blood boil. I felt my face getting hot and red. "Believe me, he's not going to be anything to me," I hissed, glaring hard at Mom for effect.

She stared back at me with the righteous glow I hated.

"I prayed about it to Heavenly Father," she said smugly. "I know this is the right decision for our family."

Mom, who had converted to Mormonism as a teenager while still living in Austria, was convinced she received revelations from God and prayed about every little decision she made. It drove me crazy that she acted like God was calling the shots for her because it made it impossible to argue with her.

I wanted to scream at Mom. Instead, I shot her a final glare and stomped out of the room.

I may have just turned thirteen, but I could see the situation for what it was. Earl was a homeless, smelly fake who was pretending to be a good Mormon so Mom would marry him and he could mooch off of her. I knew Mom was desperate for a husband and for a temple marriage to a priesthood-holding Mormon man, but this was insane.

They set the date for March first, which was the soonest they could schedule a marriage in the Mormon temple. Earl started spending evenings and weekends at our house. He didn't say much to us kids and we didn't say anything to him. Most of the time, he and Mom stayed locked in her bedroom reading scriptures together. I knew it was all part of his ploy to make Mom think he was as religious as she was, and it made me sick.

The first Friday in February, Dad dropped by for an unexpected visit. It was early evening, and as usual, Earl was hanging around, his grimy, yellow home-on-wheels parked on the dirt strip in front of our house.

I had told Dad all about Earl during his weekly phone calls, but my words clearly hadn't prepared him. The shock on his face when he walked in the door and took in Earl and his stench was so funny I had to bite my lip to keep from laughing.

Earl stood next to Mom in the foyer, tightly gripping her hand with his grease-stained, stubby fingers. He had just come from the motorcycle shop where he worked and still wore his navy blue mechanic jumpsuit with the name "Earl" embroidered on the pocket.

For what seemed like minutes, no one said a word. Then Dad jumped into action.

"Well, hello," he said in a booming, playful voice. "I'm the ex. You must be my replacement. Hope you're better at obeying than I was."

5

Earl didn't speak; he just tightened his grip on Mom's hand. Mom glared at Dad, who grinned and shot her a look that I interpreted as a "You traded me in for that?" glance.

"Dis is Earl," she said finally. Watching them interact reminded me of how Dad used to tease Mom by having her repeat the words "Thirty-third Street," where they used to live, because it came out "Turty-turd" Street. But that was back when they still got along and laughed together.

Mom and Earl quickly retreated to the kitchen with my two-year-old brother, Daniel. Jacob, Mom's obedient favorite, trailed behind them. That left Dad to visit with Connie, Heidi, and me in the living room.

"Well, that was interesting," Dad said, shaking his head. "I don't know what's gotten into your mother. But then again, she always was a little cuckoo."

"At least you don't have to hang around him and smell him every day," I lamented. "He's disgusting."

My sisters and I started telling Dad more about Earl and his fake Mormon act, but I noticed he wasn't listening. He kept fidgeting on the juice-stained green couch the church had donated to us and glanced repeatedly at the front door.

Dad never could stay in one place for long because he couldn't stand being caged. He also had a short attention span for everything but work. He was obsessed with becoming a millionaire and was always on the lookout for a business opportunity that would finally make him rich.

"Well," he said about ten minutes into the visit, "the real reason I stopped by is because I'm heading to Albuquerque, New

Mexico, for a weekend business trip. I'm wondering if any of you kids want to come with me."

I felt like I had just been handed a Get Out of Jail Free card.

"I do!" I yelled excitedly, throwing my arms around him for a hug.

Dad was an independent salesman and was always going on road trips. I escaped with him anytime I got the chance because when I was with him, I felt free.

I'm sure Dad already knew that I would be the only one to accept his invitation. Jacob never left Mom's side and my sisters couldn't stand spending long hours cooped up in the cab of his truck or sitting through his never-ending business meetings. But I loved it. I understood Dad's need to be free and to create his own destiny. I thought he had the perfect life and wanted to be just like him.

Dad and I also had another thing in common: We hated Mom's obsession with the Mormon religion, which she forced down our throats every minute she got.

Along with dragging us kids out of bed every morning for an hour-long session of scripture reading, hymn singing, and prayers, she made us pray six or seven times a day. And on Sundays, she wouldn't even let us change out of our church clothes or turn on the TV.

"You know that God believes in free agency and that forcing people to do something is from the devil, don't you, Ingrid?" Dad said to me once while I was tagging along to one of his meetings. "But that's exactly what your mom does. I remember once I was home on a Sunday and decided to go to a

Sacrament meeting. Afterward, I'd had enough and was headed out the door and you know what your mother did? She and another lady from church each grabbed me by an arm and dragged me into a Sunday school class. I went and didn't say anything, but you know how bad that turned me off? I never went back again.

"Your mom thinks you kids are supposed to be dictated to and forced into a certain way of thinking," he continued. "She treats me like that too. She thinks salesmen are the lowest form of scum on Earth. She wants a husband that goes to a nine-to-five job every day, is home every night, and sits next to her at church. But I'm not about to be a slave—to her or to anyone else."

After I jumped at the opportunity to go with Dad to New Mexico for the weekend, both Connie and Heidi quickly declined. Connie said she had to take care of Abbey, the pure-bred Irish setter she had recently purchased with money she'd saved from her maintenance job at a nearby park. Heidi, who was ten, said she had stuff to do.

I was secretly glad they weren't coming. It meant I would have Dad to myself.

"Well, Ingrid, I guess it's just you and me," Dad said with a smile. "We've got a lot of miles to cover and need to get going, so you better go tell your mom."

I jumped up off the couch and raced through our dirty, whitewashed hallway to the kitchen. I found Mom standing beside Earl next to our fold-out kitchen table.

"Mom, Dad invited me to go with him to New Mexico for the weekend. We need to leave in a few minutes. Is it okay? Can I go?"

My question was really just a formality. I couldn't imagine that Mom would have a problem with it. Though she had been granted sole custody of us by the court, she never prevented me or the other kids from spending time with Dad.

She hesitated for a moment and then looked over at Earl. "You'll have to ask Earl," she said.

I felt the blood draining from my face. She actually wanted me to ask him for permission to go somewhere with my own dad?

I shot Mom a pleading look, but she wouldn't return my gaze. She kept her eyes trained on Earl.

I turned to face him, struggling to maintain my composure. Hot adrenaline was pumping through my body. I felt such an intense rage surging inside me that it was everything I could do to keep from punching him.

Earl looked at me with his icy cold eyes. A small, mean smile crept across his face.

I sucked in some air, trying to calm myself.

"Can I go with my dad to New Mexico for the weekend?" I seethed. Earl paused for a long minute, and I could see his mind churning.

"I don't know," he answered finally, gloating as he spoke. "Your mother and I are going to have to pray about it."

I stared incredulously at Earl. His smile widened.

I turned to Mom. "Mom, please. Can I please go with Dad? He's waiting for me." I concentrated on keeping my voice calm, determined to hide the panic building inside me.

She ignored my imploring looks and gazed at Earl. As a priesthood holder, Earl was supposed to have a direct line of communication with God. Dad had been kicked out of the church, which meant his powers had been taken away.

"We're going to have to pray about it," she repeated. Then the two of them headed to her bedroom and closed the door.

I ran back to the living room to report the situation to Dad, who was still sitting on the couch, waiting. I was shaking and fighting to hold back tears as I spoke. Dad looked as if he were ready to blow.

"What the hell does he have to do with this?" Dad fumed, punching the couch with his fist. "What in the hell is wrong with your mother?"

We both waited on the couch for Mom and Earl's answer. My stomach was churning. I couldn't believe this was actually happening.

A few minutes later I heard them come out of Mom's bedroom. I followed them down the hall to the kitchen to hear their answer.

"What about church?" Earl asked smugly. "You have to go to church."

I glared at him, channeling all my hatred his way. He knew Dad had been excommunicated and wouldn't want to go. He also had to have realized there wouldn't be any time. Dad said Albuquerque was 550 miles away from Logan, our small northern Utah town. We had just enough time to get there, go to his meeting, relax a little, turn around, and come back.

I ran into the living room.

"Dad, they say I have to go to church. Is there a way we can find a church in New Mexico?"

Dad's face turned purple. "Tell them whatever the hell they want to hear!" he barked.

I headed back down the hall to the kitchen.

"Dad says he will make sure that I attend at least one church meeting," I said, directing my comments to Mom.

I felt smart and victorious.

Earl didn't say anything for a minute. Mom stayed silent.

"Your mother and I will have to pray about it some more," he said finally. Then he grabbed her by the hand and led her back to her bedroom.

I swallowed the screams making their way up my throat as I headed back to the living room to report the news to Dad. He didn't speak, but his hands were clenched into fists.

I took my place next to him on the couch to wait. My stomach felt like a hundred bees were buzzing inside it, angrily stinging me as they bumped up against their prison walls. My thoughts were racing so fast I couldn't focus on any of them. I could see my hands trembling, and I wanted to reach out and hold Dad's hand for support, but he looked too angry to touch.

After what seemed like hours, Mom and Earl emerged from the bedroom a second time. Once again, I headed for the kitchen.

"Well?" I asked, holding my breath.

"Ingrid," Earl said, a wide smile breaking open across his face. "I'm sorry, but the answer is no. The Lord doesn't want you to go with your dad at this time."

The emotions that had been bottled up inside me came rushing out. "Mom, please let me go," I begged between sobs. "This is important to me. Please!"

11

She didn't say anything for a minute. She just stood silently next to Earl.

"You heard what Earl said," she replied finally, avoiding eye contact with me. "The answer is no."

I turned to face Earl.

"Earl, I want to go with my dad. He's my DAD. I have a right to be with him."

His eyes danced. It was clear he was savoring every moment of this.

"I'm sorry, Ingrid. I really wish I could let you go. But like I told you, the Lord said, 'No.'"

I ran back to Dad, sobbing as I relayed the news.

"That's just bullshit!" he yelled. "Bullshit! Bullshit! Bullshit!"

Dad's face turned the bright purple color that always signaled an oncoming explosion. He jumped up from the couch and stormed to the front door, slamming it behind him without even saying good-bye to me.

I ran to my attic room and shoved my dresser against the door as a barricade. I flopped down and leaned against it, sobbing, trembling, trying to make sense of what had just happened.

I spent the next hour crying. Then the tears stopped, and slowly a new hardness took hold of me. I grabbed my journal and pen and scribbled the words "I hate Earl" over and over across the pages. I wasn't sure what was coming next. But as I sat there in the growing darkness, I made two vows to myself: I was never going to let that psycho religious fake rule me again. And this was the last time either he or Mom would ever keep me from being with my dad.

2

. . .

B. E. (Before Earl): Fall 1975

Before Earl showed up at our door, I didn't think things could get much worse for our family.

Dad was gone all the time, we were flat broke, and the fighting between him and Mom had escalated to the point that my sisters and I often locked ourselves in the bathroom for protection when they started in on each other.

My first real inkling of the troubles in our family started when Mom suddenly yanked us out of school and moved our family to Mississippi during the fall of my third-grade year.

"If your dad wants to work out there, then that's where we're going," she announced in a flat, defiant tone one morning after scripture reading. "We're supposed to be together as a family— not living thousands of miles apart."

I knew from *The Book of Mormon* stories and other church

lessons that Mom forced on us each morning that Dad was supposed to be at home, watching over us and guiding us with his priesthood powers, not living on the road as a salesman. I also knew how upset this made Mom because she was always accusing him of abandoning us. But the only thought that repeated through my eight-year-old mind was that Dad got to leave all the time and I was stuck at home. And Mom's announcement made me feel like I'd just won the lottery.

"This is the best day of my life!" I shouted, ignoring the deep frown creasing her face as I did a jig across the living room floor in my nightgown. Mom arranged for a neighbor to look after our Utah house while we tried out our new life in Mississippi. A few days later, we stuffed our duffel bags and plastic garbage bags full of clothes into the trunk of her rusted brown Buick and were on our way.

I started begging Dad to take me on a road trip the minute we arrived in Walls, an ugly Mississippi border town located about twenty miles from Memphis, Tennessee. And after two relentless months, I finally got my wish.

"Well, Hippie Boy, it's just you and me this weekend," he said, chuckling as he watched me crawl into the cab of his brown Dodge pickup. "What do you think about that?"

Dad called me "Hippie Boy" because my long, often tangled brown hair reminded him of the hitchhikers he picked up during his road trips. But he said it was also because, with my spunk and determination, I should have been born a boy. He didn't have a nickname for any of the other kids and I viewed it as proof that he loved me best.

Everything about Dad attracted me. I thought he was as

handsome as a movie star. He wore his strawberry-blond hair combed back against his head like Elvis, and had warm hazel eyes that were so big I could sometimes catch my reflection in them. When he smiled, his entire face lit up and he had a loud, booming voice that made people listen. I heard Grandma say he had the golden tongue because he could talk his way in or out of anything.

I was proud to be Dad's daughter. I loved it that he was his own boss, made his own rules, and was working his way to becoming a millionaire—which he said was only a matter of time now. Everything about his life appealed to me, and I wanted it desperately.

As a self-employed salesman, Dad got to come and go as he pleased. He spent his time traveling the country, sleeping in motel rooms, and eating in restaurants. When he came home for visits, he often showed up in a new truck or van he had talked the local dealership into giving him for no money down. And he always dressed nice. When he wasn't in a suit, he wore jeans, a nice button-down shirt, and real leather cowboy boots.

Mom was the opposite of Dad. She rarely smiled and had a meek, quiet voice that was hard to understand even without her thick Austrian accent. She dressed in frumpy clothes she bought from the church thrift store, and never had the money to buy us new clothes or take us out to eat. Sometimes, when she couldn't afford groceries, we had to go to the church welfare office for food.

I hated being poor. But what I really hated was Mom's addiction to religion. She was obsessed with making sure our family all made it to the Celestial Kingdom, which Mormons believed was the highest kingdom in heaven. When we weren't at school or doing chores, all we ever did with Mom was read scriptures, pray, sing hymns, and go to church.

I couldn't stand our life. Neither could Dad—which is the main reason he left all the time.

"You want to know something, Ingrid," he often said as he packed his bags to leave on another sales trip. "Your mother is a religious fruitcake. And two days is about all I can take of her."

Dad turned the truck onto the highway and for a few minutes we drove without speaking. I was busy soaking in the clean, vinyl smell of his nearly new truck and enjoying my view from the high front seat. It was the Saturday after Christmas—two weeks before my ninth birthday—and this trip with Dad was the best gift I could have been given.

"I tell you what we're going to do," he said after a while, a grin breaking across his face. "Let's you and me splurge and get a nice motel room. We'll find a Holiday Inn and really live it up this weekend."

I was so happy I considered pinching myself to make sure it was real. My plan was falling into place perfectly. I knew we would be staying at a motel somewhere and I had hoped Dad would suggest someplace special like the Holiday Inn. I just needed one more thing for our weekend to be perfect. I crossed my fingers before I spoke.

"Do you think we could order room service?" I asked, holding my breath.

Dad smiled. "For you, Hippie Boy, I'll do it. It's our weekend, isn't it? First though, we're going to have a meeting with a new saleswoman I recently hired. She's really dynamic. You're going to love her, Ingrid."

I nodded in agreement. But I was barely listening. My head was swimming with thoughts about the relaxing, luxurious escape that awaited us. I had stayed in a Holiday Inn only once in my life and I knew the rooms were nice. I thought about my eleven-year-old sister, Connie. Dad had invited her to come on this trip too. But all she cared about was her animals and had stayed behind to hang out with the hamsters she'd gotten for Christmas. She was going to die of envy when I told her about our weekend.

I spent most of the five-hour drive planning our weekend. First, we would have to find a Holiday Inn, which Dad said wouldn't be a problem because Baton Rouge was a good-sized city. Once there, I was going to request a room on the top floor so that we had the best view and the longest ride in the elevator. The minute we got to our room, I was going to grab the room service menu and remote control, hop on the bed nearest the TV, and pile the pillows behind me. Dad and I would figure out what we wanted to eat, and then he would order while I studied the *TV Guide* and flipped through the channels.

Our TV at home was an ancient thirteen-inch black-and-white box. If we wanted to change channels, we had to walk over to it and turn the knob, and half the time we couldn't get a decent picture no matter how much we fiddled with the rabbit-ear antenna sitting on top of it. I couldn't wait to kick back with a remote control and bask in the clear blue and red glow of the screen.

Connie and our six-year-old sister, Heidi, were probably cleaning the house right now or helping Mom make a hamburger casserole for Sunday dinner. Other than the occasional fifteen-minute breaks Mom allowed, they would work all day. In the morning, after sitting through an hour of scripture reading and prayers at home, they would put on the embarrassing flower-patterned maxi dresses Mom had made for each of us and head to church for another three hours of religion.

I would sleep in and watch some cartoons. When I got hungry, Dad and I would order room service again—probably a stack of pancakes with whipped cream. Both of these were sins in Mom's eyes. She said Sunday was Heavenly Father's day, which meant no watching TV, no shopping, and no fun of any kind.

Dad and I arrived in Baton Rouge around 5 P.M. and headed to a local pizza parlor to meet his saleslady. Normally I would have been thrilled at the thought of eating pizza. But I had been counting on room service and was craving a cheeseburger and French fries. Just thinking about the cheeseburger made my stomach growl.

I considered asking Dad if I could skip the pizza and wait for room service. But I didn't want to sound ungrateful. I swallowed my disappointment and decided I would make up for it by ordering a banana split hot fudge sundae from room service once we settled into our motel room.

The restaurant smelled of cigarettes and pepperoni, and the lights were dim. But Dad immediately spotted his saleslady sitting at a corner table in the back of the room.

He rushed toward her and she popped up out of her seat. They greeted each other with a hug.

"Ingrid, I want you to meet Patricia," he said proudly, squeezing her arm as he spoke.

"Hi," I mumbled, suddenly feeling shy.

"Well, it's so nice to finally meet you," she said in a soft, smooth voice that carried only a hint of a Southern accent. "Your dad has told me a lot about you."

I felt my cheeks turning red—not from embarrassment, but from joy that Dad had told her about me.

"And this is my son, Ben," she added, motioning to a black-haired boy sitting next to her.

Ben nodded his head in my direction. He had black curly hair, large brown eyes, and acne that covered his forehead. He looked to be twelve or thirteen and seemed much more mature than the third-grade boys in my class.

I turned my attention back to Patricia. She wore a sophisticated navy skirt with a cream-colored blouse that spotlighted her pretty blue eyes and wavy, shoulder-length chestnut hair. With her heels on, she was almost as tall as Dad. She was as thin as some of the models I'd seen on magazine covers. In fact, she was pretty enough to be a model if she wanted to be.

We ordered pizza, and Dad and Patricia spent the next hour talking business while I stole glances at Ben. He rarely looked up from his food and didn't smile the entire time we were there. He seemed to be upset that his mom had made him come to the dinner.

We finished eating just after 6 P.M., which I figured still gave us plenty of time to get settled into our room and enjoy our evening. But as soon as we got into the truck, Dad announced that we were heading to Patricia's apartment to finish up their sales meeting.

A wave of panic shot through me.

"Do you think we should find our motel room first and check in?" I asked, trying to keep my voice calm. "I just want to make sure the rooms don't get sold out."

Dad patted my leg.

"Ingrid, you are something else, you know that? Don't worry. We'll have plenty of time to get checked in to our motel and relax. You know it's important that I finish this sales meeting. It won't take more than an hour." My face started to burn. I wanted to tell him he wasn't being fair and demand that we get our motel room first. But I didn't dare say anything more because Dad had a bad temper. I knew if I pushed too hard, he would explode and I would never get to go to the Holiday Inn.

We pulled up to Patricia's apartment building. The truck clock read 6:20 P.M.

I took a deep breath and tried to think positive. I knew we were cutting it close, but if we were back in the truck by 7:30, we would still have time to check in to our motel, order dessert, kick back on our beds, and enjoy a few shows.

Patricia met us at the door and flashed a big smile at Dad.

"Ben," she called down a short hallway. "Why don't you take Ingrid into your room and the two of you can watch TV for a while?"

"That's okay," I managed quickly. "I like listening to my dad's sales meetings. I do it all the time."

I didn't feel comfortable hanging out in some strange boy's room. Plus I wanted to stick near Dad so I could remind him when it was time to go. "Ingrid, listen to Patricia," Dad said sternly. "We're going to be talking a lot of business and it will be easier this way."

Patricia walked me to Ben's bedroom. He was sitting on his twin bed in a cluttered tiny space watching TV. He glanced up at his mom and glared. I could tell he didn't want me hanging around and was as annoyed as I was about the whole setup.

"It'll just be for an hour or so," Patricia said in a voice that sounded like a plea. Then she and Dad headed for the living room and shut the door.

I plopped down on Ben's bed and stared at the black-and-white TV sitting on top of his dresser. I didn't want to watch his stupid TV. It was as small as ours was at home. All I could think about was the time being wasted. Every minute here meant one less minute relaxing with Dad in our motel room.

I felt weird being in Ben's room. I knew I was invading his space.

"So what do you think they're talking about in there?" I finally asked, trying to break the ice.

"Who knows," he replied with a shrug, keeping his eyes glued to the TV. "They're probably doing whatever it is they always do in there."

It was clear he didn't want to talk to me, so I stopped trying to make conversation.

Every couple of minutes, my eyes locked on the clock radio sitting on an end table next to Ben's bed. I willed it to hit 7:30 so Dad would be done with his meeting and we could get out of there. But when the long hour finally passed, Dad didn't appear.

"I'm going to go see what's taking them so long," I mumbled.

I left the room and paced the hall that connected with the living room, trying to decide if I should knock on the closed door. I knew Dad would get angry if I interrupted his meeting. But I wasn't sure how much longer I could stand it. We were running out of time.

I returned to Ben's room and waited through another long hour. I kept my eyes glued to the short hallway, begging with my mind for the living room door to open. At 8:40 P.M., I couldn't take it anymore. I was in the hallway, ready to knock on the living room door and tell Dad we needed to get going when the door opened.

"Well, there you are, Ingrid," Dad said, pretending to be surprised. "Guess what? Patricia just offered to let us spend the night here. Wasn't that nice of her?"

He might as well have punched me in the stomach.

His words sucked all of the air out of me and for a minute, I couldn't speak. When I did find my voice, it was quivering and small.

"But, Dad, I thought you said we were going to get a room at the Holiday Inn."

"I know, but it's late and it'll be hard to find a motel room. And this way we save some money."

"But what about room service?" I pleaded. My heart was pounding so hard it felt like it was going to break through my chest.

"It's probably closed by now anyway, and like I said, this saves us a lot of money."

Dad shot me a look that warned me not to press the issue any further.

I fought back the scream making its way up my throat. A volcano of tears rushed to my eyes, ready to explode. But there was no way I was going to let either Dad or Patricia see me cry. I bit my lip to hold it all in and tried to keep my body from shaking as I followed him into the hall next to her bedroom.

Patricia was busy pulling out a pillow and blankets from a nearby closet. She started to apologize for not having a bed for me, but Dad interrupted.

"This is just fine. Isn't it, Ingrid?"

I stared at the floor and nodded my head.

Patricia spread out a sleeping bag on the floor and then smoothed a blue flannel blanket over it. She handed me the pillow.

"Are you sure you are going to be okay out here?"

I nodded again. Dad gave me a quick squeeze. Then the two of them said good night, flipped off the hall light, and disappeared behind her bedroom door.

As soon as they were gone and I was hidden by the darkness, I stopped biting my lip and let the tears come. I was burning with anger, but I was also so crushed I could barely breathe.

I couldn't believe Dad had done this to me. It was like I didn't even matter to him.

I thought about him in the bedroom with Patricia. I knew he wasn't supposed to be in there with her and I knew Mom would freak out if she ever found out about it. But that part didn't matter near as much as him ditching me.

I could hear Dad and Patricia whispering and laughing—not caring that I was alone on a hard wooden floor in a dark hallway, suffering from what I was sure was a broken heart.

I curled into a ball on the sleeping bag, rocking myself as I thought about all the times I had pleaded for Dad to take me with him. This wasn't the first time he had broken his promise to me. The summer after first grade, after weeks of begging, Dad agreed to take me on a two-week road trip with him. I had spent hours packing for the trip, rummaging through my drawers in search of the perfect outfits. When it was time to go, I noticed that Dad had a salesman with him, which meant that I had to sit in the backseat of his car and listen to them talk business. I didn't care, though. I was with Dad and that was all that mattered.

About two hours into our drive, Dad told me he had a special surprise for me.

"So guess what we're going to do, Ingrid?" he said, turning to talk to me for the first time since we had left. "We're going to go visit your uncle Mitchell. Doesn't that sound like fun? You can visit with your cousins."

I didn't want to visit my uncle. I hardly even knew him. On top of that, he had three little boys ages four, two and a baby, and I wasn't in the mood to hang out with toddlers. But since I didn't have a choice, I figured I would handle it for a few minutes.

We were somewhere in Idaho when Dad turned the car off the highway and drove down a long, isolated dirt road. At the end of the dusty road was my uncle's mobile home. I saw him open the screen door and walk toward us.

"How's it going, Mitchell?" Dad said, stepping out of the car. "You remember your niece, don't you?"

The two of them talked for a minute. Then Dad turned

toward me. "So, Ingrid, I've decided I'm going to let you visit with Uncle Mitchell and your cousins for the next couple of weeks," he said, acting like it was a special treat for me. "I know your aunt could really use the help with your cousins and it will be a nice visit."

I couldn't believe what I was hearing. He couldn't be serious.

"No!" I yelled, panic sweeping over me. "Dad, I want to go with you! You promised!"

There was no way I was going to let him dump me off at my uncle's trailer in the middle of nowhere.

"Ingrid, I want you to listen to me," Dad said, his voice suddenly firm and impatient. "It's too hard to have you on the road with me. I want you to stay with your uncle and I want you to listen to him and be good. I'll be back to get you in a couple of weeks."

That's when I noticed that my uncle was holding my polka-dotted suitcase. I burst into tears.

My uncle grabbed my hand.

"Now, Ingrid. It's going to be fine," he said.

Dad was back in the car and already starting to drive away. I broke free of my uncle and started running after him. Dad just drove faster. I could hear my uncle yelling for me to come back. I was sobbing, frantically calling after Dad to stop and come get me.

Dad's car tires kicked hot dry dust into my tear-soaked face and mouth. But I kept on chasing after him. I ran until I couldn't see his car anymore and then sat down on the road and sobbed. A minute later my uncle caught up to me and offered me ten dollars if I would please just stop crying and come back to the trailer with him.

I had hated every second of those two weeks and had sworn then that I would never let Dad pull something like that on me again. Now here I was, stuck on some stranger's floor—once again tricked, ripped off and humiliated.

Until the sleepover at Patricia's house, I thought our new life in Mississippi was going great. Dad still came home only once or twice a week, but it was much better than the once-a-month visit we had when we were living in Utah. And moneywise, things seemed to be looking up.

The house Dad rented for us was small, only about nine hundred square feet, and the front yard was noisy because of all the cars and semitrucks whizzing by on the four-lane highway next to it. But it was new. And compared to our ancient, run-down house in Utah, it was luxurious.

The minute we pulled up to the curb in our dirty, rusted brown Buick, I sensed things were improving. I raced into the house with Connie to check things out.

The first thing I noticed was that the narrow, closet-sized kitchen had its own dishwasher, which meant Connie and I didn't have to scrub dishes anymore. The eating nook next to the dishwasher opened into a family room with new cream-colored, wall-to-wall carpet.

"Connie, you have got to come here and check this out," I yelled. "It's got a fireplace!"

I had always dreamed of a fireplace and I loved the way my

feet sunk into the soft plush carpet. At home, our carpet was so old that some areas were worn bare to the plywood floors beneath it. It was like walking on cement.

The other side of the kitchen led to a small, rectangular living room, which featured the same cream-colored carpet. At the end of the living room was a short hallway that opened to three small bedrooms, with a bathroom sandwiched between the first two. Mom and Dad's bedroom had its own bathroom.

"This is great!" I squealed as I examined the kids' bathroom. "It even has a shower in it!"

Connie and I equated having a shower and two bathrooms to being rich. Our house in Utah had only one bathroom and an old claw-foot tub that looked like it belonged in the 1800s.

The two of us quickly staked out the room we planned to share, the one located in the corner at the front of the house. That left Heidi and my brother, Jacob, with the smaller middle bedroom next to Mom and Dad's.

Mom didn't seem nearly as excited when she walked through the house. Later that afternoon, when Dad headed across the border to Memphis to meet up with his sales crew, she started to cry.

She called us all into the room with the fireplace for a talk.

"You have to be very careful whenever you are outside," she told us, her eyes swollen. "You can't go into the street. It's too dangerous. And your dad says the swamp next to it has alligators in it, so don't go near there."

Mom was desperate to find a Mormon church. We didn't have our phone connected yet, so we all piled into the car in search of a pay phone. After driving around for a while, we found a 7-Eleven.

"I'll be back in a few minutes," Mom said, stepping out of the car. "I don't know if it's safe here so roll up the windows and keep the doors locked while I'm gone."

We watched her walk across the parking lot and enter the phone booth. When we left Utah the week before, there had already been snow on the ground. Here, it was still warm and humid, even though it was the first week in November. With the windows shut, the air in the Buick was suffocating and smelled like dirty socks.

Heidi and I decided to pass the time by covering Jacob's head in tiny ponytails that stuck up everywhere. He wasn't even four yet and could be talked into almost anything.

Connie, as usual, was quiet and serious. She sat straight as a board in her privileged spot in the front passenger seat, her carefully brushed auburn hair tucked neatly behind her ear as she watched Mom through the windshield.

"Here she comes," Connie announced after about fifteen minutes. "She doesn't look happy."

I glanced up from the makeover I was performing on Jacob just as Mom opened the car door. She looked like someone had just died.

"I can't believe this," she said, her voice shaking as she spoke. "The nearest church is across the border in Memphis. That's twenty miles away."

By the time we got back to our new house, Mom was crying again and shut herself into her new bedroom to pray.

At home in Utah, there were two Mormon chapels within a four-block radius of our house. It was weird to think we would have to drive to a new state just to go to a church meeting. I was secretly glad to have a little distance. But I knew it was a serious blow to Mom because the church was like her family.

Mom had told us her conversion story more times than I could remember. I wasn't crazy about the religious part. But I was so fascinated by her childhood that I never got tired of hearing her talk about it.

Mom had told us she was born in Graz, Austria, in the fall of 1940, just when World War II was really getting started. She was the only child of a police officer, whom she loved dearly, and a mean stepmother who hated her and made Mom sell her only doll to get money for alcohol.

The reason her stepmom hated her so much is because Mom's real mother had fallen in love with her dad while he was married and had gotten pregnant with Mom.

"I don't know if I was wanted," Mom had told us, the sadness blanketing her voice when she spoke. "My father was silent about my birth and never said anything about my blood mother, not a single word. But the story I heard from my stepmother was hurtful. She would say, 'Your mother is very, very bad and you are going to be as bad as your mother. She forced your father to have a baby and now we have you—an ugly little disgrace!'"

As a child, Mom said she had no idea that her blood mother was only seventeen when she had given birth to her, and that when Mom was still a baby, her mother had been working for the Resistance Movement and had been captured by the Nazis. It wasn't until Mom was an adult that she'd learned the truth.

"It turns out that during the first five years of my life, my biological mom had been locked up at Ravensbrück, a concentration camp for women," Mom told us, pausing to explain that concentration camps were horrible prisons where Hitler sent millions of people to be killed or to work as slaves. "My mother nearly starved to death in there, and she was so sick and weak that her body was full of worms. Right before the Americans came to liberate the camp in1945, she was taken on a death march. The prisoners walked for miles and if they couldn't keep up, they were killed by the guards. My mother was so weak, she started having a hard time moving and was stabbed with a bayonet and left for dead.

"She was thin as a skeleton when a Red Cross doctor found her, and though she was only twenty-two years old, all of her hair had turned white from malnutrition. It took nearly a year before she was healthy again. At that time, she was given a choice. She was told she could go back to Austria or start a new life in France. She chose France."

Had Mom known the truth about her blood mother, maybe she wouldn't have felt so alone and unloved as a child. But all she was told was that her real mom didn't want her. And though her stepmother was occasionally kind to her, she got so mean when she was drunk that she sometimes locked Mom in a room and threatened to kill her with a knife.

"Along with selling my toys and being forced to go to the taverns and beg them for liquor for my stepmother, my earliest memories are of sirens, bomb shelters, and dead bodies," Mom had told us, continuing her story. "When I was four, I remember running into a bomb shelter with my dad, my stepmom, and another family. There was a big explosion and we were all knocked out. When I woke up, I saw that the other family was dead. And when we came out of the shelter, there were dead people everywhere and the apartment we lived in was just a pile of rubble. Everything we had was gone."

Mom's dad, who had worked as a police officer and then a security guard, contracted tuberculosis when she was still a young girl and spent most of Mom's childhood sick in bed. Mom kept to herself at school and often just sat and cried at her desk. Because she was poor, the other kids teased her. And even if she had wanted to have friends over to her apartment, her stepmother wouldn't allow it. So Mom would stand by the window of her third-story apartment and watch other children play.

Mom told us the only time she felt loved and happy was at church. She was Old Catholic and loved the rituals. She also craved the peace she felt on Sundays, sitting in the chapel. Once a week Mom was allowed to attend religion classes and the vicar paid special attention to her. He became Mom's best friend and confidante. Recognizing her passion for religion, he even talked to her about going to a school to teach religion.

Teaching religion was Mom's dream, but her stepmother wouldn't allow her to pursue it because her family needed money. After finishing school at fifteen, she was forced to find a job at an engraving shop. That was Mom's life for the next year, until one day her stepmother surprised her by saying that Mormon missionaries from America had stopped by for a visit and that she had invited them back to meet Mom.

"I was sixteen at the time and felt like I knew all the answers," Mom said. "I had read the Bible from the beginning to the end, so I felt like I had sufficient knowledge of religion and was prepared to defend my belief."

Mom planned to put the Mormon missionaries in their place.

But as soon as they told her about the Mormon religion, she said she felt in her heart that they were speaking the truth. She was also struck by the fact that the elders were so sure of their testimony and of the truth of the Mormon religion.

The only thing Mom struggled with was the Joseph Smith story—about how Heavenly Father talked directly to him, and had chosen him as the prophet who was to restore the only true church, which had been lost over the centuries.

"I felt that if Heavenly Father truly lives and he actually talked with Joseph Smith, then he would also speak to me," Mom explained stubbornly. "I mean, why not?"

On the advice of the Mormon missionaries, Mom had read *The Book of Mormon*, gave up coffee and tea because it's against the Mormon religion, and started praying nightly for an answer. On her third night of praying, she said she finally got the affirmation she needed.

"Suddenly I felt a burning sensation and indescribable joy in my heart, and I knew without a doubt that God lived because I felt his presence. So now I could ask him the question about which church was true: Was it the Church of Jesus Christ of Latter-Day Saints or was it the Catholic Church? Then I received the answer—it was a voice coming from across the room where the elders had taught me the gospel. The voice quoted a scripture from *The Book of Mormon*, and in that moment, I knew God had answered me. I couldn't deny it."

The day after arriving at our new house, Mom and Dad went to a secondhand store in Memphis and bought mattresses, metal bed frames, and dressers for us. The rest of the rooms were left bare until my uncle could bring out some of our junky, mis-matched furniture from home. I preferred it this way because I didn't have to be embarrassed when I had my new friends over. At least for a while, I could make up some excuse about Mom not having the time to go furniture shopping.

There wasn't much to see or do in Walls. It was flat with a lot of big cotton fields and swampy areas—not at all like the moun-tains that surrounded Logan. Mom loved the rugged Wasatch Mountains at home because they reminded her of the mountains in Austria. But I was fine with our new surroundings. I could just stay inside and enjoy our fireplace and dishwasher.

After giving us a few days to adjust, Mom took Connie and me to enroll in our new school. Heidi, who had just turned six in early September and had started first grade at home, wasn't even allowed to attend school in Mississippi because she missed the first grade cutoff date by a week and they didn't have kindergarten.

At home, we could walk to our elementary school. Our school in Walls was five miles away from our house and so big it looked like a high school. It was two stories tall and took up nearly an entire block.

Mom sighed as she parked the car.

"Okay, stay close to me," she said as we headed into the building.

It was in the middle of the day and the halls were empty. We found the school office and met with the secretary, who gave Mom a stack of papers to fill out and told her important infor-mation about which school bus Connie and I would need to ride.

Then she directed her attention to the two of us.

"Our school goes from first grade to eighth grade," she said in a slow, lazy drawl. "You two are still in elementary school, so ya'll will stay on the first floor."

I was fascinated by her accent and mimicked it all the way back to the car.

"Stop it right now!" Mom barked, looking like she was ready to lose it. "When you talk like that, it makes you sound stupid."

I was so shocked I couldn't speak. Mom never used words like "stupid." To her, that word was as bad as swearing.

The next morning Mom drove Connie and me to our new school and told us to go to the office so they could walk us to our new classes.

This time, the halls were crowded. That's when we noticed all the black kids.

I had only seen one or two black people in my life. Though Mom taught us to be kind to everyone, we believed God was punishing black people with dark skin here on Earth to pay for their behavior in the spirit world, also called the Pre-Existence. That's where we believed all of us—Satan and Jesus included—lived as spirit children before being born. As a result, black people were banned from entering the Mormon temple and black men couldn't hold the priesthood. It would be two and a half more years before church officials would lift the ban, citing a new revelation from God.

"I'll bet we're the only Mormons," Connie whispered as we made our way to the principal's office.

Connie preferred to keep to herself and didn't like being put in the spotlight. I knew she was nervous about starting a new school because she kept fidgeting with her glasses. But I couldn't wait. It was my chance to become someone different.

The office secretary walked us through the crowded halls to our classes. She stopped at mine first and opened the door.

"This is I-n-g-r-i-d," she announced in her slow drawl. Then she left.

I did a quick scan of the room and noticed what seemed like an invisible line dividing my new classmates. All of the black kids sat on the left side of the class; all of the white kids sat on the right side. They were all staring at me. And no one said a word.

There was still about five minutes before the opening bell and my new teacher hadn't yet arrived. I had to do something to break the ice.

"Bet none of you know how to spell 'Phyllis,'" I announced from the front of the room. Phyllis was my best friend in Utah and I was proud to know the secret trick to spelling her name.

"Can too," several of the white students yelled.

"Okay, let's see it—write it down, but don't show each other."

I waited a minute and then began making the rounds from desk to desk in the white section, checking my classmates' work and gleefully announcing that they were wrong.

"It doesn't start with an 'F,'" I finally revealed. "Phyllis starts with a 'Ph.'"

Just then my teacher came in and called the class to order. I felt happy and relaxed as I sat down at the desk he assigned me amid my new white friends. This was going to be fun.

The only bad part about my new school was that the teachers

hit kids when they misbehaved. I saw it happen in the hallway my first day there. That same day, I noticed that the principal had a wooden paddle sticking out of his back pocket.

"It's got nail heads hammered into it so it stings more when he hits you with it," one of my new friends warned me at lunchtime. I decided I didn't want to find out if they were telling the truth, and vowed then and there to always call my teachers "ma'am" or "sir" and follow every class rule.

After school ended each day, Connie and I met in front of the building and caught our school bus home. In Utah, Tuesday afternoons were reserved for Primary, a church meeting for kids. But since the nearest church was so far away, Mom couldn't get us there in time, which meant that we got a break from any weekday church activities. Mom still made us get up at six most mornings to read scriptures, but we didn't have a piano so we skipped some of the hymn singing. And when Dad was home, we sometimes skipped our morning church sessions altogether. Mom also let up on homemaking projects such as sewing and bottling fruit for food storage when Dad was around. We still had our chores, but those weren't bad because having a dishwasher made cleaning the kitchen a piece of cake. With no furniture and only a few toys to deal with, the rest of the house never seemed to get messy.

Life finally felt good.

I cried for what seemed like hours before finally falling asleep on Patricia's floor. But I was already awake when she opened her bedroom door.

"Did you sleep okay?" she asked. Her voice was kind and she wore a concerned look.

I was still stinging from the night before and my eyes were almost swollen shut from all the crying I had done, but I was determined not to let on.

"Yeah, I slept fine," I mumbled under my breath.

She invited me into the kitchen for a glass of milk. I followed her into the room and sat down at her round kitchen table. She wore a pink bathrobe and her hair was tussled, but she still looked pretty. She pulled a plastic cup from a cupboard, filled it with milk, and set it down on a place mat in front of me.

"So what do you sell with Dad?" I asked her, trying to make conversation as I sipped my milk. It was real milk, not the lumpy powdered milk we drank at home, and it tasted good.

"Calculators," she said. "Want to see one?"

"Sure."

She hurried from the room and came back minutes later holding a black leather rectangle in her hand. She pulled out the calculator and laid it on the table.

"You can go ahead and play with it if you'd like."

The calculator excited me. Dad never let me touch the calculators in his inventory. He said I might break one. I cradled it in my left hand, caressing it as I slid it out from its black leather case and ran my fingers over the smooth, cool buttons. I studied them carefully. There were the regular numbers and math signs, but there were also symbols I didn't recognize.

"Do you want it?"

I looked up and saw Patricia watching me. She looked pleased. I stared at her in disbelief. This was an expensive calculator. I figured Dad could probably get seventy or eighty dollars for it. A debate kicked off in my mind. I knew I was supposed to say "no thank you," but my fingers kept brushing over the buttons and I couldn't keep my eyes off the smooth black leather case.

"Yes," I said quickly before I lost my nerve. "I would love it. Thank you." She smiled and patted my head. I ran to the hallway and buried the calculator in my duffel bag before Dad woke up and saw it.

My hurt from the night before started to fade. Getting a calculator was almost as good as spending a night at a motel. We stayed at Patricia's house the entire morning. She made us eggs and bacon for breakfast and offered me a knowing smile each time she caught my eye. I was starting to like Patricia and could understand why she was Dad's favorite salesperson.

After breakfast, she and Dad had another meeting in the living room while I watched TV in Ben's bedroom again. This time, I didn't even mind.

Dad and I left Patricia's house around noon to start the long drive back to Walls. For the first hour, we drove in silence. My thoughts were on my new calculator, carefully tucked away in my duffel bag. I was dying to get it out and examine it more closely. I couldn't wait to show Connie. She was going to die of jealousy.

Dad started the conversation.

"You know, I don't think you ought to say anything to anyone about where we spent the night. Patricia's my saleslady and she was nice enough to offer us a place to stay so we wouldn't have to spend money on a motel, but I just don't think you should say anything. In fact, if anyone asks you, just say that we went to a sales meeting, because that's really all we did."

"Okay," I assured him. "She was really nice." My gut was still aching from the whole episode and I preferred to forget about it.

Dad seemed relieved and smiled. I figured this was a good time to introduce the calculator.

"You want to see what she gave me this morning?" I asked.

I could feel myself glowing as I reached into my duffel bag and pulled out the calculator. My mood changed the minute I saw Dad's face. It had turned beet red.

"You shouldn't have taken that from her!" he barked. "Do you know how expensive those are? That wasn't right. What were you thinking?"

Dad's reaction startled me. I knew he wouldn't be thrilled about me accepting such an expensive gift, but I didn't expect him to get angry about it.

"I'm sorry," I said, feeling my own rage ignite inside me.

"You can't show that calculator to anybody. Do you understand me? That was just really stupid to take that from her."

"But you broke your promise about the motel!" I wanted to scream at him. "You lied to me!"

My hands were trembling and I felt my lower lip quiver. I knew I was about to explode so I nodded my head in response and then quickly turned to stare out the window. I spent the next thirty minutes pretending to be engrossed in the road signs. I knew it was wrong to accept such an expensive gift, but it was the one good thing out of the entire trip.

Dad broke the silence.

"Well, I wish you hadn't taken the calculator," he said, his voice now patient and kind. "But since you did, you need to promise me that you won't show it to anyone or say anything about where you got it. Do you understand?"

"Sure, Dad," I mumbled.

I closed my eyes and pretended to be asleep for the rest of the drive. As soon as we got home, I hurried to my room with my duffel bag and shoved it under the bed. Nobody asked me about my trip so I didn't have to say anything. The next morning, Dad left to meet up with his crew in Memphis.

I wanted to keep my promise to him, but I was dying to play with my calculator and show Connie. When she and I were alone in our bedroom, I decided to let her in on my secret.

"You want to see something?" I asked her. "You have to promise not to tell anybody though."

"What?" Connie asked.

I walked over to our bedroom door and shut it tight. Then I knelt down on the floor and retrieved my duffel bag from its hiding place. I reached into the bag and pulled out the black leather case that held the calculator. Slowly, I slid the calculator into my hand. Connie's eyes looked like they were going to pop out of her head.

"Where did you get that?" she asked accusingly.

"Dad's saleslady gave it to me," I answered. I could feel a grin spreading across my face. "We spent the night there and in the morning she surprised me with it."

Connie suddenly had this weird, shocked look on her face, and I knew I had screwed up big time.

"You've got to swear you won't tell anyone about this—either about the calculator or spending the night at Dad's saleslady's house," I said quickly. "I promised Dad I would keep it a secret."

I was in my room, playing with my calculator, when Mom stormed in a few hours later. The look on her face scared me.

"Ingrid, I want you to tell me right now what you and your dad did over the weekend!"

"I didn't steal it, Mom. I promise. Dad's saleslady gave it to me."

Mom acted as though she didn't hear me. She grabbed me by my arm. "Let me say it again," she hissed. "I want you to tell me exactly what you and your dad did while you were gone!"

I had never seen Mom so angry. She looked like she was going to hit me. I took a deep breath and started at the beginning. When I got to the part about spending the night at Patricia's house so we could save money on a motel room, she dropped my arm and stormed out of my room, slamming the door behind her.

Dad came home the next day, and he and Mom started screaming at each other. Then he left again and Mom announced we were moving back home.

"Thanks for ruining my life," I wanted to snarl at Connie when we were alone in our room. But I couldn't prove she told Mom, and I felt so guilty I wanted to shut it all out of my mind.

A few days later, we stuffed our duffel bags and trash bags full of clothes into the trunk of our Buick, piled into the car, and started our two thousand mile trek back to Utah. Despite our ruined weekend getaway, I would have done anything to stay near Dad and our new, nice house. I dreaded going back to our suffocating, miserable existence at home.

I couldn't shake the sick feeling in my stomach as I sat crammed in the backseat with my brother and sister. I knew it was my fault we were moving back to Utah, and I knew Dad knew it too. We hadn't even talked since that weekend, and I was worried sick that he was mad at me. I didn't know when I was going to see him again and I was convinced he'd never want to take me on a trip with him again.

3

. . .

Back in Utah, life quickly returned to the way it was before we left.

Except that a dark cloud now hung over our house.

Mom started locking herself in her room to pray for hours at a time and smiled even less than before. And Dad stayed away for nearly two months before he finally came to visit us. I was sure he was still mad at me for telling Mom about Patricia because when I met him at the door, he didn't give me a hug or swing me around like he usually did when he arrived. He just walked into the house and headed straight for the living room couch.

I followed behind him, pulled off his cowboy boots, and brought him a glass of water, same as I always did when he arrived.

"How was your trip, Dad?" I asked nervously. "Did you have a good drive?"

He didn't answer. He just stared at the large living room window in front of us like he was in a daze.

I plopped down beside him, waiting and hoping for him to snap out of his bad mood.

The seconds of silence crawled like hours.

"You know something? I'm tired," he said finally. "I'm gonna go take a nap."

"Sounds like a great idea," I agreed quickly. "I'll bet you'll feel a lot better when you get up."

I wrapped my arms around him for a hug, but he only half hugged me back. He pulled himself off the couch without saying another word and headed for the bedroom. When he emerged a few hours later, he was dressed in a suit and tie and left with Mom for what I overheard her tell Connie was a church trial.

When I woke up the next morning, Dad was gone.

I felt a lump in my gut that only got bigger when Mom called us all into the living room for a family announcement.

"Last night, your dad was excommunicated from the church," she said quietly. Her voice was flat and dark circles hung below her bloodshot eyes. "This means he's no longer a church member."

I could hear the hurt and shame in Mom's voice and though she didn't look at me, I was certain she was blaming me for the whole mess.

We all knew Dad had to do something really sinful to get kicked out of the Mormon religion. I was sure it had something to do with Patricia because at church the week before, I overheard Mom telling one of the sisters that Dad had committed adultery. I knew adultery was against the Ten Commandments and that it tied back to Dad sleeping in Patricia's bedroom.

"So does this mean you and Dad are getting divorced?" Connie asked bluntly.

My heart jumped when she said the words. Mom said nothing for a minute.

"No," she sighed, though her voice didn't sound the least bit convincing. "Your dad and I are going to try to work things out."

Getting Dad kicked out of the church was bad enough, but causing a divorce was more than I could handle. I didn't need Connie giving Mom any ideas. I didn't understand why she even brought it up until later that day, when she explained to me that since Dad was no longer a church member, Mom's temple marriage to him was no longer valid.

"Just think about it," she prodded, rolling her eyes like she always did when she was impatient or annoyed. "If they don't have a temple marriage, they aren't married for time and eternity, and can't be together in the Celestial Kingdom. So what's the point of them being married at all?"

I hadn't considered this and she had me worried. But after mulling it over, Connie said I should chill out.

"Don't sweat it," she said, rolling her eyes again—but this time in an all-knowing sort of way. "They're not going to get divorced because Mormons don't get divorced. And Mom's the best Mormon around."

It didn't occur to either of us then that without Dad, Mom had no family. Mom had been an eighteen-year-old nursing student when she'd met Dad at church in Austria, where he was serving a two-year Mormon mission. By then she had already been living on her own for two years and had such a burning desire to move to the United States that she had already applied for a visa. Mom had no family to speak of—she had still not met her blood mother, and within months of meeting Dad, her father died of tuberculosis and her stepmother went crazy and was locked away in an insane asylum.

Dad, then a nineteen-year-old farm boy from Utah who dreamed of doing something big with his life, said he knew he wanted to marry Mom the minute he saw her.

"I tell you what, Ingrid. Your mom was real pretty back then," he told me once when I asked him how they met. "I remember walking into church one Sunday and seeing her standing there all dressed up in her nursing uniform and hat. She was something else. She was so determined and smart, and she was so petite. I don't think she weighed more than a hundred pounds."

They wrote letters to each other while Dad finished out his mission. Even before he returned to Utah, he sold his bike and begged relatives for the rest of the money to buy Mom's airplane ticket to the United States. As soon as she graduated from nursing school, Dad flew Mom to Utah. Shortly after, the two of them married, and Dad's family became Mom's family. Without him, Mom was alone.

I noticed people staring at us the next Sunday at church. But no one said anything to me and nothing changed at home. When Dad called a few days later, he sounded happy again.

"How's my Hippie Boy doing?" he boomed with a laugh. I felt his voice smiling through the receiver and relief washed over me. Dad sounded like his old self. He didn't seem upset anymore—either about being kicked out of the church or about Mississippi.

"Hey, Dad! How's it going? Where are you? When are you coming home?"

Dad mistook my desperation for excitement and got a chuckle out my anxious inquiries.

"You are something else, you know it?" he said, which was the same thing he always said when he called. "I'll be home before you know it. And then you and I are going to have a great time, okay?"

"Okay," I managed, reluctant to hang up the phone. "But promise me you'll hurry."

I clung to Dad's voice like it was a life raft, hoping he could save me from my existence.

It wasn't just the nonstop church sessions and chores, or the suffocating sadness that clogged the air around me. It was also the depressing, run-down state of our house.

Mom insisted on keeping all of the walls in our house white because she said white represented good and helped keep Satan out. But they hadn't been painted in years—making them a dirty grayish color—and the plaster was crumbling in some spots, leaving big, gaping holes right down to the wooden beams that held our house together. To cover up the holes in our flower-patterned living room carpet, Mom used mismatched kitchen rugs she'd purchased from the church thrift store. They made the floor look like a patchwork quilt and were the first thing anyone noticed when they came to our door. I hated it all, but I was especially bothered by our kitchen.

Aside from the cubby space that housed our stove, sink, and fridge, the room was just a large rectangle with a peeling yellow linoleum floor. Most of the space was taken up by a banquet-style plastic table, with water-damaged black vinyl chairs that Dad had scavenged from a flood in Idaho.

Jammed into one corner of the room was a giant aluminum trash can that stored our fifty-gallon bag of powdered milk. On the other side of the table sat our washing machine, which also doubled as counter space and a cutting board. Sometimes food crumbs slipped into the cracks around the lid and got washed with our laundry. No one else I knew had a washing machine in their kitchen and I found it mortifying. But even worse than the washing machine was the laundry hamper that sat next to it, only two feet from our table. The laundry smelled up the kitchen and flies were constantly swarming around the room. They got so bad during the warmer months that Mom hung a long yellow fly strip from the light above the kitchen table to catch them. Every once in a while, a sticky dead fly dropped off the strip and landed in our food while we were trying to eat.

When I asked Mom if we could move the fly strip somewhere else, she looked at me like I was crazy.

"Flies are attracted to food," she explained matter-of-factly. "So the best spot for the fly strip is over the table."

In the back of my mind I knew it was partly Dad's fault that Mom was sad and that we didn't have any money. But it was impossible for me not to associate her with chores, church, and being poor. And the only break we got from any of it was when Dad came home.

As soon as he walked in the door, a different energy took over the house. Mom's rules and home church sessions went away. So did her food, usually, because Dad didn't like the Ship-wreck Stew or other meals Mom managed to pull together on our small grocery budget. He often surprised us with a bucket of Kentucky Fried Chicken.

"Look what I got," he would say as he placed the steaming bucket of fried chicken on the center of the kitchen table. "Who wants to dig into this with me?"

Dad usually came home on a Saturday and I always spent the fifteen-minute breaks Mom allowed us between chores stationed at the living room window, watching for his truck to pull up. When he finally arrived, I made sure I was the first one to run out and greet him.

"Dad!" I would yell as I rushed into his arms for a hug. "You made it! I missed you to the moon and the stars and back."

"Well, look at you, Hippie Boy." He would laugh as he wrapped his arms around me. "I think you're even prettier than you were the last time I saw you."

Our routine was always the same. I would walk him into the house and wait impatiently by his side while the other kids lined up for their hug and kiss. Then I would drag him by the hand to the couch in the living room and spend the next few minutes snuggling next to him, telling him about my life and bringing him snacks from the kitchen.

Dad couldn't stand being away from his work for very long and after about forty-five minutes of visiting with me, he always headed to the phone in the kitchen to make his business calls. I would trail behind, pull up a chair next to him, and listen to what sometimes amounted to hours of phone conversation. If Dad said he had a business meeting to attend, I insisted on going with him. If he said he was tired and needed a nap, I sat in the hallway outside his bedroom waiting for him to wake up.

After dinner, I cuddled with him in the living room again until it was time to go to bed.

Because Dad spent only a couple of days out of each month at home, I guarded him closely and wasn't about to share him with my brother and sisters—or even Mom. I figured we all needed to fend for ourselves, and if the others weren't as demanding or persistent, I concluded it was their fault.

Before moving to Mississippi, Mom had put up with my attention-hogging ways. But now that she was on a mission to save her marriage with Dad, she decided it was time to put a stop to my selfish behavior.

One day shortly after Dad arrived, she grabbed me by the arm as I was heading to the fridge to make him a sandwich. She pulled me to a corner wall for a talk.

"What you are doing is not right," she chided in a loud, harsh whisper. "You need to let your dad spend time with me and your brother and sisters. Do you understand me? You aren't the only one who matters in this house." I knew she had a point. But I wasn't about to let her make me feel guilty.

I glared at her, pulled away, and ran back into the living room to be with Dad. I didn't care how Mom or the other kids felt. I knew how I felt and how much I needed Dad. And I was willing to do whatever it took to make sure he felt the same way about me.

A few weeks later, when Dad called to say he would be home for his birthday, I decided to do something big to get his attention—as in surprise him by jumping out of a cake in a string bikini.

I had watched a sexy girl do this on TV and it was the first thing that popped into my nine-year-old mind. I didn't own anything close to a string bikini like the girl on TV wore and had no clue how to make the trick cake that was used. But I concocted a modified version that I was certain would elevate me to favorite-child status.

Early on the morning of Dad's late summer birthday, I recruited Heidi, then almost seven, to help me bake a chocolate cake. Dad wasn't due home until 4 P.M., but I wanted to make sure there was plenty of time to execute my plan.

"What I want you to do is wrap me in a box with the cake, and then I'll jump out and surprise him," I told her while we frosted the cake and carefully arranged thirty-seven candles.

I spent hours getting ready. I started by dressing in the most revealing outfit I owned, a pair of strawberry-patterned terry-cloth shorts and a halter top my cousin had recently donated. I brushed my long, auburn hair until it was smooth and glossy, and softened my lips with Vaseline. I even snuck a little of Mom's mascara to make my eyes pop.

To substitute for the confetti the girl in the bikini had used, I convinced Heidi to help me cut up the Sunday paper into thin strips. We then headed to the cellar to retrieve the cardboard box Mom used to haul around her canning bottles. Together, we dragged the box up the wooden stairs and positioned it near the front door.

At 3:30 P.M., I climbed inside the box, which was just big enough that I could sit down in it if I pulled my knees into my chest. Heidi handed me the cake pan, which I balanced on my knees. Then she shoved the newspaper strips into the cracks on either side of me.

Once that was done, she set to work wrapping the box.

"Hurry up," I urged from behind the cardboard walls. "He's going to be here any minute."

Heidi finished wrapping just before 4 P.M. and went to hide in the living room.

Ten minutes passed. Then twenty.

My legs started to cramp and the air in the box turned hot and clammy. "Heidi, I can't breathe!" I yelled. "You've got to get me some air!"

She ran to Mom's sewing room, grabbed a pair of scissors, and punched holes in the back of the box. Then she headed back to her hiding spot.

We waited. There was no sign of Dad.

After an hour and a half, Mom announced that she and the other kids were going to the neighborhood block party for some sloppy joes. I loved sloppy joes and had been looking forward to the party all week.

"Okay. I'll be over in a few minutes—just as soon as Dad gets here," I called from inside the box.

Time slowly ticked away. To keep me company, Heidi came out of her hiding spot and sat next to the box. We talked about the surprised look on Dad's face when he opened his present.

Another half hour passed before the phone rang. Heidi ran to answer it. It was Dad.

"I'm running a little late," he told her. "I should be there in a half hour or so."

Heidi decided this would give her plenty of time to head across the street for some food. I envisioned all my neighbors laughing and having a good time. Along with the sloppy joes, I knew there would be potato chips and orange soda—food we never got to eat at home.

I listened as the door shut behind Heidi and willed myself not to feel bad. I ignored my growling stomach and focused my thoughts on Dad and on how happy I would make him.

The minutes crawled.

Sweat rolled down my back and I could feel the newspaper strips sticking to my legs. I wiggled my feet to keep them from falling asleep.

Heidi returned after a few minutes. The block party ended soon after and Mom, Connie, and Jacob returned as well.

"What are you doing?" Connie asked as they filed past the box. I could feel her eyes rolling in her head.

Heidi punched a few more holes into the back of the box so I could breathe easier. Finally, at 7 P.M., Dad arrived.

"Hi, Dad," Heidi said as soon as he came through the door. "Open your present."

I waited as Dad peeled off the paper and opened the box. "Surprise!" I yelled, struggling to stand up.

I was dripping with sweat and my hair was matted against my face. The chocolate frosting had melted and dark smudges of ink from the newspaper confetti covered my thighs.

There was a long second of silence. The room was so quiet I could hear my heartbeat.

"Well, this is nice," Dad said finally.

I heard the hesitation in his voice as he eyed both me and the cake. I was suddenly mortified by my bare stomach and sweaty, ink-covered body. I didn't need a mirror to know how ridiculous I looked. I saw it in Dad's face. "I tell you what," he said, pushing past me as he spoke. "I have to make a quick phone call and then we'll eat."

I watched him head for the kitchen, leaving me standing in the box with the cake and confetti. Heidi trailed behind him, anxious to distance herself from the spectacle she had helped create.

My face flushed with shame. For a minute, I was too stung to move. I just stood there in my clammy, inky mess. I could feel the tears pressing against my eye sockets but I was determined not to let them come. I didn't want either Dad or the rest of the family to know the extent of my humiliation.

I sucked in my breath and concentrated on keeping my face blank.

I waited for a few minutes to pull myself together. Then I carefully climbed out of the box with the cake, forced my mouth into a smile, and headed for the kitchen.

The stinging feeling vanished a few minutes later, when Dad hung up the phone and gathered me in his arms for a hug.

"What do you say we dig into that cake?" he asked, a big grin spreading across his face. "I'm hungry."

4

. . .

Connie and I camped out in the hallway next to the door leading to the attic stairs. We both had our heads pressed to the wall, straining to make out the angry hissing sounds vibrating though the ceiling above us.

We mostly caught snippets of Dad's rants, because Mom's voice was too quiet to carry.

"Maybe instead of going to that bishop all the time, you ought to come to me for a little advice and support," his voice thundered through the ceiling. "Do you know how hard I work? Seven days a week! Maybe if you stopped preaching to me and started accepting me for who I was, I would want to stay at home and would have more money to give you!"

Dad and Mom now fought every time he came home for a visit, which was becoming less and less often. We hated it when they argued because Dad had a bad temper and it was hard to know what would set him off. When the trigger came, it was like watching the guy on TV turn into the Incredible Hulk. Dad's face would turn purple, the veins would bulge out of his neck, and his hands would ball into fists. Then he would blow and whatever was in his way got destroyed.

Neither Connie nor I were in the mood for an explosion. But what was bothering us most about this particular fight was that they had chosen to have it in the attic.

Connie's bedroom was in the attic. So was our TV.

Connie was irritated because she needed to get her violin so she could practice. Her orchestra teacher had a fit when students showed up unprepared and often threatened to kick them out of the class.

Connie was like that—always wanting to be responsible and do the right thing. I just wanted to watch TV.

The two of us played Rock, Paper, Scissors for a while, ignoring Dad's angry shouts and hoping he and Mom would be done soon.

When we grew tired of that, we had contests to see who could last the longest making a bridge with their body across the hallway. I always won because I was practicing to be a cheerleader when I got older and could already do the splits.

After a while, we got bored with that, too, and sat against the wall with our knees hugged into our chests, silently willing them to wrap things up already.

I picked at my hangnails, trying to pass the time. Connie was restless and grabbed a piece of paper and pens from the kitchen so we could distract ourselves with a game of dot-to-dot. By the time we were finished with that, she was fed up and ready to act.

"If I just sneak up to my room, they probably won't even

notice me," she began, adjusting the brown-framed glasses she sometimes wore. "It will only take me a second."

I was usually the daredevil in the family and I wanted to be upstairs just as much as she did. But we both knew the potential consequences far outweighed the benefits.

"I wouldn't do it," I warned. "It's going to make Dad mad."

"Yeah, but they've already been up there for two hours," Connie fumed. "What do they expect us to do?"

We sat in silence for the next few minutes, straining to hear their conversation. It was muffled, but much quieter now, and we both took this to be a good sign.

Connie spoke up.

"Mom wants me to get good grades, right? If they get upset, I'll just explain that I need to practice my violin or I'll flunk."

"I wouldn't do it if I were you," I cautioned again, though I wasn't very forceful because I was starting to rethink my position. Mom and Dad had been going at it forever, and I was beginning to wonder if they would ever be done.

We waited in silence for a few more minutes. Connie looked at me and I could tell by the expression on her face that she had run out of patience. I had too. Wonder Woman was about to start.

"I'm going up," Connie announced, pushing herself up off the floor and grabbing the doorknob.

"Okay," I said, trying to hide the relief in my voice. "Good luck."

The explosion came within seconds.

"What in the hell are you doing here!" Dad's voice blasted through the house. "Did I say you could come up?"

His rant was interrupted by a loud crashing sound. Another

scream and smashing sounds followed. I felt the familiar fear rip though my chest. I wasn't sure what was coming next and ran to the living room for cover. I immediately headed for my hiding spot in the corner crevice between the piano and couch. I huddled there, trying to keep myself from shaking. There was more yelling, crashing, and banging. Then I heard glass shattering and wood splintering.

I hugged my knees close against my chest and pushed my body hard against the side of the piano, willing myself to become invisible. I heard a final yell. Then I heard Dad's heavy footsteps crashing down the old plywood steps and the slam of the front door. The house went silent except for Connie's wailing sobs.

I was worried that Connie was hurt and felt guilty for letting her go upstairs. But I was too scared to move.

I waited until I heard Dad's truck roar away and then cautiously stepped out of my hiding spot. I rounded the corner, opened the attic door, and started making my way upstairs. The first thing I noticed was that the half wall that lined the top of the stairway was busted apart and now hung in pieces of jagged wood. When I reached the top of the stairs, I saw that our TV was on the floor with a big hole in the screen, surrounded by shards of broken glass. Mom's bookshelf was overturned and books were scattered across the floor.

Connie was standing in a corner clutching her black violin case. She looked small and scared. Mom stood with her back to me, a few feet in front of her.

"I was just trying to get my violin," I heard Connie pleading in between sobs. "I wasn't doing anything wrong."

I never heard Mom's response because she suddenly realized I was standing there.

"Ingrid, go back downstairs. Now!" she ordered.

I moved slowly down the steps, straining to hear more, but the only noise I heard was Connie's muffled sobs.

During Dad's next visit home, he and Mom fought in the living room. This time, Connie and I knew better and locked ourselves in the bathroom. Heidi and Jacob hid in a small room tucked away at the back of the house. When the front door again slammed and everything went quiet, Connie and I tentatively made our way down the hall to the living room.

My eyes locked on the new light fixture that Mom had proudly purchased a few months before. It had a long, brass neck that branched out into six arms, each featuring a pretty white glass cup that held a lightbulb. What we had affectionately referred to as "our new chandelier" was now a mass of broken glass dangling from ceiling wires.

Then I saw the piano—the used Wurlitzer Mom had spent years dreaming about and had purchased two years earlier on a five-dollar-a-month rent-to-own plan. Connie must have seen it at the same time because she made a gasping noise that sounded a lot like a dog's yelp. Half of the piano keys were chipped from the force of Dad's fists pounding on them. The piano bench looked like it had been karate chopped. Pieces of wood lay scattered across the living room floor, mixed in with the hymnbooks that had once been stored inside.

My eyes moved from the piano to the couch where Mom sat, tears streaming down her face.

"Are you okay, Mom?" Connie asked, running to her side to comfort her.

For a second, I couldn't speak. I couldn't believe Dad had ruined Mom's piano. What was wrong with him?

I took a seat on the other side of Mom and hugged her. Mom just sat and sobbed—harder than I had ever seen her. I couldn't tell if she was crying because she was scared or had a broken heart.

"It'll be okay," I heard Connie say, doing her best to be the support system she always was to Mom. I wanted to agree with her but I couldn't. Everything in the room was busted up or torn apart—just like our family.

How could things ever be okay?

I had a hard time reconciling the Dad I worshipped with this crazy man who petrified me. I began to escape by locking myself in my room with the wire hook lock that hung on the door. Once safely inside, I would lie down on my bed, close my eyes, and dream about my real family—the Osmonds—who would soon come to take me away.

I settled on the Osmonds because they were rich, famous, and Mormon—plus, I figured they already had so many kids that throwing me into the bunch wouldn't make a difference.

My fantasy was always the same. There had been a horrible mix-up in the hospital nursery on the day I was born and I had been given to the wrong family. For years the Osmonds had been secretly looking for me. They couldn't advertise it because they didn't want hundreds of kids coming out of the woodwork claiming to be theirs, so it was taking longer than it should have. But any minute now, I expected them to knock on the door and save me.

I imagined how angry Donny would be when he discovered

that his little sister had been living in such awful conditions. Once rescued and driven the hundred-mile journey by stretch limo to the Osmond compound, he would take me into his room—which I knew from reading *Tiger Beat* magazine could only be entered through a tunnel—and sit me down on his bed. I envisioned it would feature a purple quilt since purple was Donny's favorite color.

"I'll never let anyone hurt you or treat you like that again," he would fume, putting his arm around me protectively and holding me close.

Wrapping up our private talk, the two of us would make our way back through the tunnel and out into the living room. That's where all of my other brothers and my sister, Marie, would smother me with hugs and tell me how sorry they were for losing me. I would pretend to be angry at first, just so they knew how hurt I was. But then I would melt from their love and affection and tell them that I forgave them.

After feasting on a celebration dinner at a fancy restaurant nestled against the mountains in Provo, Utah, we would head back to the Osmond compound where a surprise would be waiting for me. My new parents would walk me into my bedroom— a big, beautiful room with delicate wallpaper featuring tiny purple violets and plush, cream-colored carpet. In the center of the room would be a large, four-poster bed with princess curtains and a white, lace-lined down comforter. Amid my squeals of delight, Marie would come into the room, gently take me by the hand, and lead me to my walk-in closet, which would be packed with Calvin Klein jeans, thick, hand-knitted sweaters, and a dozen or so pairs of Cherokee-brand shoes.

My daydreams were so vivid they began crossing over into real life. I started making daily phone calls to an Osmond Ranch I had located in Paradise, Utah, hoping that Donny, Marie, or their youngest brother, Jimmy, would answer. I was so sure the Osmonds were coming for me that I sat glued to the *Donny & Marie* show each week, and then headed down to the cellar where Mom stored our church-recommended food supply to mimic their songs. As the youngest and newest Osmond, I figured I would be joining the Donny and Marie act and I wanted to be prepared.

Connie, also an Osmond fan, was disgusted by my near perfect delivery of "Paper Roses," Marie's signature song.

"You know, you could get sued for copying her like that," she bellowed once when she caught me mid-act. "They have copyright laws!"

I ignored her and kept singing. Inside, I was ecstatic. I knew I sounded good and her protests only confirmed it. When my family came for me, I would be ready.

5

. . .

"Ingrid! Connie! Come to the kitchen now!"

Dad's angry, thundering voice triggered a panic button inside me.

My nine-year-old mind started spinning and racing through the past week, trying to remember what I had done wrong. Nothing was ringing a bell, but from the sound of his voice, I was sure we were in trouble.

"I said come to the kitchen!"

I raced to the room, fighting the urge to throw up. Connie, now twelve, came scurrying down the living room hallway and arrived at the same time. Our eyes locked for a second and I saw my fear mirrored in hers. We both turned toward Dad, who was pacing next to the table and looked like a lion ready to pounce.

"Go get your shoes on," he ordered. "You two are doing the grocery shopping."

For a second I felt relieved. Dad was angry, but he didn't

seem to be angry at us. Then the weight of his words sank in. He wanted Connie and me to do the grocery shopping.

Mom never allowed us to pick out food from the grocery store. She always planned our meals ahead of time from the *Meals on a Budget* recipe book she'd been given by one of the sisters at church. She made a detailed grocery list before leaving the house so she knew exactly what she needed and wouldn't make an impulse buy that she would regret later.

I shot a nervous glance at Connie and then looked at Mom. She was sitting near the end of the kitchen table. The blood had drained from her face and I could see tears bubbling in her eyes. As soon as she saw me looking at her, she turned away.

Dad pulled a hundred dollar bill from his wallet and handed it to Connie.

"Here. This ought to cover it."

I eyed the crisp, green bill Connie was now clutching and heard myself gasp. In my nine years, I had never seen that kind of money.

I looked at Mom for some sign of approval. Her lower lip was quivering.

"Jerry, you can't let them do the grocery shopping. That money has to last us the entire month." Her voice was quiet and pleading.

Dad didn't respond. Instead, he turned back to Connie and me. "I said to go get on your shoes. I'll meet you both in the truck."

I didn't dare look back at Mom. We ran to our rooms, grabbed our shoes, and hurried outside.

It was only an eight-block drive to the grocery store, but it felt like an eternity. I was seated in the middle next to Dad and could feel his heat. I glanced at Connie, who was staring out the passenger window, pretending to be interested in the houses we passed.

I wanted to ask basic questions, such as "How much hamburger should we get?" and "Do you think it would cheer Mom up if we picked up some ice cream?" Instead, I concentrated on my hands, trying to force them with my mind to stop trembling.

Dad pulled into the grocery store parking lot and drove up to the glass doors.

"I'll pick you up in a couple of hours," he said.

We took this as our cue to get out. As soon as Connie slammed the truck door shut, Dad hit the gas and drove off.

I couldn't get the image of Mom out of my head. I saw her sitting at the table, tears running down her cheeks. I could hear her pleading with Dad not to give us the grocery money.

I didn't want to hurt Mom. But I didn't dare defy Dad. I was scared. But Connie, who had recently started seventh grade, seemed perfectly fine. She flipped her feathered brown hair over her shoulder, marched through the automatic glass doors, and headed straight for the line of grocery carts.

She grabbed one and motioned for me to do the same.

"We've got a lot of groceries to buy," she explained patiently, as though she had done this a million times. "This way, we make sure we have plenty of room for everything.

"Don't worry about it," she added, seeing the panic on my face. "This is our opportunity to show Mom that we are responsible."

She smiled and I immediately understood that there was a hidden meaning to her words. This was also our chance to get some food we liked.

I started to relax a little. Maybe Connie was right. Maybe we could do a good job and make Mom happy.

I followed her up the first aisle, helping her to scan the shelves for the no-name products like Mom always did. Connie told me the secret was to look for the ugly packaging and to check the bottom shelves, where she said most of the no-name brands were hidden.

"It's all the same food," she explained, acting like she had been to cooking school. "The only thing you're paying for are the labels and fancy pictures."

I didn't know how Connie knew so much about food, but I was grateful that she was taking charge.

Truthfully, Connie and I didn't really have that much in common anymore. Since starting junior high a couple of months before, she had joined the volleyball and basketball teams and was always at practice or at a game. And when she wasn't doing that, she was hanging out with her pet rabbits or the animals at Willow Park, a small nearby zoo. It was like she was turning into a jock or something—which was the complete opposite of the cheerleader I still envisioned becoming soon.

The first aisle was packed with deli meat and crackers, and aside from grabbing a large box of saltines, we skipped over everything there. The next row in was the cereal aisle. Here, Connie paused.

"I don't know about you, but I'm ready to take a break from Cream of Wheat," she said, a sly smile creeping across her face.

"Definitely," I said, starting to get excited.

I moved my cart to one side of the aisle to get it out of the way and took my time scanning the wall of cereal boxes. My eyes first locked on a jumbo box of Fruit Loops. That's what I really wanted. But I knew they were too expensive and that getting them would upset Mom. I also craved Cocoa Puffs, but I forced my eyes to pass on those too.

"How about something like Cheerios?" I offered finally.

"Good choice," Connie said. We scanned the bottom shelf until we came across a two-pound plastic bag labeled Toasted Oats and tossed it into my basket.

The next aisle over, we picked out ten boxes of Hamburger Helper, and grabbed several bags of egg noodle pasta. We also stocked up on cans of no-name French beans, peas, and tomato sauce.

Now that I was in the swing of things, I was having fun and starting to feel confident about our grocery shopping abilities. I trailed behind Connie, carefully weaving my cart through each aisle, ignoring the quizzical looks from the moms we passed.

In the meat section, we selected three five-pound family packages of ground beef—23 percent fat because Connie pointed out that the higher the fat content, the cheaper the meat. At the dairy section, we picked out two eighteen-pack cartons of eggs. And in the vegetable section, we selected a head of iceberg lettuce and a twenty-pound bag of baking potatoes.

Then it was time for the frozen food section.

Our mouths watered as we eyed the ice cream and frozen pizzas, which we forced ourselves to pass. But when I spotted the potpies, my favorite food, I stopped.

"I think we should get these," I said to Connie, preparing to argue my case. "I mean, each of them is a meal by themselves and they are easy to make."

I loved potpies—especially chicken potpies. Once or twice a year, Mom surprised us with them. I loved that they were each in their individual packages, which meant that we could eat them directly from the tin. I also loved the thick, creamy broth, the chunks of chicken, and the way the peas and carrots tasted like the broth itself. But the best part was the piecrust. I was always careful to save the crust for last. I would make a small hole in the top of the potpie, just big enough for my spoon, and eat out all of the broth, chicken, and vegetables. Then I slowly ate the crust, letting it melt in my mouth. Just thinking about it made my stomach growl.

"Please, Connie," I continued. "They're so good and they don't use up any dishes, which means cleaning the kitchen will be easy on the nights we eat these."

It didn't take much convincing. We pulled out ten of them, ensuring we had enough for two dinners. We also decided that a large bag of tater tots made good dinner sense and tossed those into the basket.

On Connie's advice, we skipped the bread aisle because just across the parking lot was a Wonder Bread Outlet. It's where grocery stores took bread that couldn't be sold because the loaves had been squished or had exceeded the expiration date stamped on the bottom of the bag. But they were always at least half off the regular price.

The checkout clerk eyed us suspiciously as she rang up our groceries but she didn't say anything—even when Connie handed her the hundred dollar bill. She returned a five dollar bill and change to Connie, who tucked the money into her front pocket. Then the two of us walked our carts jammed with food over to the Wonder Bread store and pushed them just inside the shop, where we could keep an eye on them.

I followed Connie to the bread section that covered the back wall. "Look, Ingrid," she said, motioning to the sign by the bread. "Ten loaves for one dollar! Mom is going to LOVE this."

All of the ten-cent loaves were at least a week over their expiration date. We picked through them carefully, leaving behind the ones that felt hard and stale when we cupped the bags with our hands. We decided to go for all ten loaves, figuring Mom could store some of them in the deep freezer we kept on the back porch. Satisfied that this buy alone would put a smile on Mom's face, we headed for the checkout counter. On the way, we passed by the fruit pies.

"I think we earned one of these, don't you?" Connie said with a smile. I nodded and we quickly added two cherry fruit pies to the basket.

Connie paid for the bread and fruit pies with the five dollar bill left over from the main grocery excursion, ignoring the checkout clerk when she suggested that our mom wouldn't want us bringing home stale bread. Then we added the loaves of bread to our stuffed shopping carts and headed back across the parking lot to wait for Dad.

We sat down on the curb and sank our teeth into our fruit pies.

"Now aren't you glad that Dad asked us to do the shopping?" Connie asked as we slowly savored our fruit pies.

Dad's Dodge pulled up soon after we had finished.

He stepped out of the truck to help us load the groceries. I was relieved to see a smile on his face.

"Well, look at this," he said, eyeing the two carts filled with grocery bags. "It looks like you girls did just fine. I knew you would. Your mother's always talking about the need for faith. Maybe she just needs to have a little more faith in you."

We pulled up to the house and Dad unloaded the bags from the truck. Then he drove off and left Connie and me to haul in the grocery bags ourselves.

My stomach was back to knots as I trailed Connie into the house with two bags of groceries, placed them on the kitchen table like Mom always did, then returned to the lawn to grab some more bags.

Mom came out of her bedroom to see what the commotion was. Her eyes were red and swollen.

I was so nervous I was ready to throw up the cherry fruit pie I'd just devoured.

"I tried to pick out the same kind of food you usually get and made sure we bought all no-name brands," Connie said in a calm, upbeat voice. "And I think you are going are really love the bread deal we found. Ten loaves for only one dollar. Do you want to see what we got?"

"Not right now," Mom said quietly.

She left the kitchen and went back to her bedroom.

I stared anxiously at Connie, who still seemed calm and in control. "Don't worry about it," she said in a soothing, assured tone. "Mom's still upset but everything will be fine. Let's surprise her by putting everything away."

A couple of months later, Mom called us all into her bedroom for what she said was a "big surprise."

I was excited. Maybe she would say we were moving again. Or tell us that we were finally going to get a dishwasher. I entered the room and found her sitting on the worn gold bedspread that covered her bed, wearing a goofy smile on her face. She looked so happy she was glowing.

We all crowded around her, anxious to hear her announcement.

"Well, children. I've got some exciting news." She paused for a moment to let her words sink in. The room was so silent I could hear my heart beating.

"I'm pregnant."

If my siblings responded, I didn't hear them. I was so shocked by Mom's words I couldn't focus.

This was definitely not the surprise I had in mind.

Her two-word announcement washed over me, and then began seeping in through every pore. She was having another baby. This meant another kid to take care of, another mouth to feed, another person to share what little we had.

"What are you thinking?" I wanted to scream. "You don't even have enough money to take care of the kids you've got!"

Was I the only person who had any sense around here?

Every week I watched Mom as she sat down to pay the bills and felt her stress as she tried to determine which bills to skip. Dad's deal with Mom was that he would wire her one thousand dollars a month, which rarely happened. But even when he was able to meet his commitment, there was never enough money to go around. Before anything else, Mom gave her 10 percent tithe to the church, figuring that if she paid God first, God would take care of her. This left her with nine hundred dollars to work with for the month—when she was lucky. Each week, she took out her recipe box where she stored the bills and spread the papers out over our fold-out kitchen table. The one bill she always paid was our eighty-seven dollar mortgage payment because she wanted to make sure that we didn't lose our house. From there, it was a crapshoot. If it was winter, she made sure she paid the gas bill so that we had heat, but sometimes the electricity got turned off. Aside of the hassle of going without our stove and washing machine, I didn't mind this so much because we got to use flashlights and candles. But it was a pain in the summertime because that's when Mom was likely to skip the gas bill—which meant we had to heat water in a big pot on the stove whenever we wanted to wash up.

The phone was always the first thing to go because Dad often ran up huge long distance bills during his visits home. Once, Mom got so fed up with him for always causing her to get the phone disconnected that she had a pay phone installed in the foyer leading to the living room. Then she secretly hooked up a regular phone in her sewing room and kept it hidden in the closet.

"Don't tell your dad about it or we'll lose it," she warned us.

When Dad arrived home, walked in the house, and saw the pay phone, he came unglued.

"What the hell is this?" he yelled.

"We couldn't afford a phone anymore because of your calls, so our only choice was to put in a pay phone or not have a phone at all," Mom answered smugly.

Dad dropped his bags in the hall, stormed back out of the

house, and headed to the grocery store for a roll of quarters. When he came back, he pulled a kitchen chair next to the pay phone and began making his calls.

He used the pay phone until that evening, when he heard the regular phone ringing from the sewing room closet. I was scared he was going to blow up, but he remained surprisingly calm.

"You know, I think your mother's a little sick in the head," he announced with a sigh. Then he took the phone out of the closet and started dialing. After that, the pay phone was useless so Mom had it removed.

I was tired of worrying about how Mom was going to take care of us. It was stressful and embarrassing. When our toilet broke, we spent nearly three weeks peeing in our backyard garden and knocking on our neighbor's door when we needed to do a number two before Mom was able to pull together the money to hire a plumber. We never got to buy new clothes. They were either all hand-me-downs from my cousin or secondhand clothes from the church thrift store. And every week at school, I had to go through the humiliation of being called up to my teacher's desk to get my free lunch tickets.

"Who is having hot lunch this week?" she would ask the class each Monday morning, counting the raised hands so she could get a tally for the lunchroom cooks.

Then she would pull out two white envelopes from her desk. "Ingrid and Nanette, here you go," she would say.

Nanette and I were the only ones in our class who got free lunches. My teacher never said the envelopes contained lunch tickets. But it didn't take a rocket scientist to know what they were. I could hear some of the kids in my class snickering when I walked up to her desk to grab the envelope. I wanted to crawl into a hole and die.

Sometimes, when money got really tight, Mom couldn't afford groceries and had to call the church welfare office. They provided her with vouchers to pick up free food from a large brown warehouse. I felt like Mom had paid for the groceries plenty of times over with her tithing money, but it was still mortifying to go there and pick out food while the warehouse manager watched us. It was even worse for Connie because Mom made her help the church janitor clean to work off the food donations we received.

After Mom's surprise announcement, she ended with a prayer, just as she did for every family gathering.

"Our dear Heavenly Father," she said. "We want to thank you for all of your blessings and especially, Heavenly Father, for sending this new special spirit to us."

Her prayer droned on for a few more minutes, but I stopped listening. In my head, I was saying my own prayer. *Please, Heavenly Father, please let this all be a mistake.*

Daniel was born in late August, just before I started the fifth grade. Dad came home to witness his arrival. A few days later, he left again. Money was so tight that Mom—who was determined to be a homemaker like all the other women at church—finally broke down and started a daycare in our house.

I arrived home from school one day to a living room packed with crying, snot-nosed toddlers. The room stunk of dirty diapers and sour milk, and as soon as I entered the house, Mom roped me into a round of diaper changing. This meant rinsing soiled cloth diapers in the toilet and figuring out how to pin down squirmy kids with one hand so I didn't accidentally stick them with safety pins when I put on their clean diapers.

The routine lasted most of my fifth-grade year and I couldn't stand it. Mom must have tired of it too, because as soon as the school year ended, she gave up on the whole homemaker fantasy and landed a job at the County Health Department as a public health nurse.

Mom's new job consisted of making home health visits to elderly patients in the valley, checking in on them, taking their blood pressure, changing their catheters, and inserting IVs. Because it had been ten years since she had worked as a nurse, Mom was nervous about sticking needles into people's arms to get the IV going. She practiced on oranges for a while, but she worried that she wasn't getting it right so she came up with a solution.

She called Connie and me into the kitchen and made us an offer.

"I need to practice on people," she explained. "If you two let me practice on you, I'll give each of you a quarter every time I stick you."

Connie, who had just turned fourteen, was finally eligible for a job through Manpower, an employment agency that put low-income kids to work. She had recently landed a job caring for animals at a park located about a mile from our house and wasn't about to get tortured for a measly twenty-five cents.

"You're kidding, right?" she asked, rolling her eyes. "You've got to be out of your mind."

With that, Connie turned and walked out of the kitchen, leaving just Mom and me. I didn't like the idea of being jabbed with needles either. But I had already started adding up the money in my head and envisioning all the trips I could take to the candy store, a corner gas station located only four blocks from our house. The promise of instant cash for a few seconds of pain seemed worth the trade off.

"I'll do it," I said, rolling up my sleeve so she could get started.

Mom practiced on me over the next two weeks. She would dot a cotton ball with alcohol and rub it mid-arm, where my veins were most prominent. Then she would tie a rubber tourniquet just above the spot she was targeting to cut off the blood flow and make the vein pop. On the count of three, she would insert the needle, trying to get it into the heart of the vein.

Sometimes Mom missed the vein altogether and had to start over. It hurt, but I prided myself on having a high tolerance for pain and I never made a sound.

By the time Mom was done practicing, my right arm—which housed the biggest veins—had needle tracks resembling a drug addict. Fortunately, summer was about to start and I wore long-sleeved shirts the remaining week of school so no one noticed.

6

· · ·

For the first time since the Mississippi fiasco, I felt free and was having a little fun.

With Mom working full-time at the Health Department, and Connie putting in thirty-two hours a week at her park job, I was now in charge at home.

"I really need your help this summer," Mom had confided a couple of weeks before school ended. "What I need most is for you to take care of Daniel. But you'll also need to keep an eye on Heidi and Jacob and make sure work gets done around the house. Can you handle the responsibility? I'll pay you a dollar a day."

My eleven-year-old brain went into overdrive. A dollar a day for five days a week was twenty dollars a month, plus the occasional quarters I was paid when Mom wanted to get in more practice drawing blood.

My insides were buzzing with excitement over the pile of money that awaited me.

"Of course I can handle it," I replied, making my voice sound as mature as I could. "Don't worry, Mom. I've got it under control."

I had already babysat a couple of times for a lady at church, and between that and helping Mom care for all the toddlers in her makeshift daycare for the past year, I knew I was plenty capable of caring for Daniel, who was now ten months old. I figured Heidi and Jacob could look after themselves. Within a week of summer break, I had the home routine down pat.

Mom still got us out of bed at 6:30 to read scriptures and eat breakfast as a family. But then she and Connie were gone and the day was mine.

"TV time," I would call to Heidi and Jacob as soon as the door shut. We would grab our pillows, plop down onto the living room floor, and spend the next two hours soaking up *Gilligan's Island* reruns and whatever else we could find on the three channels we could get.

Once Daniel was up, I changed him, made him a bottle of milk and put him on the floor in the living room—shutting all the doors in the hallway so he couldn't crawl far.

As much as I had been against the idea of another sibling, I adored Daniel. He had thick red hair, hazel eyes, and deep dimples that erupted over his chubby face when he smiled. And he rarely cried or made a fuss. He just hung out, and was so mellow and good-natured that we all wanted to be with him. Every day I spent hours bathing, feeding, and rocking him. In the afternoons, I carefully buckled him into his stroller and walked him up and down our block, humming lullabies until he fell asleep.

Before she left each day, Mom taped a list of chores with our names on it to the end of the kitchen table. Heidi and I had most of the workload. Our jobs included cleaning the kitchen, washing and folding laundry, vacuuming, and occasionally washing the floors. Jacob, who was now six, only had to put away the laundry.

Heidi and I soon figured out that if we started our chores by 4 P.M., we could have them done by the time Mom arrived home at 5:30. Even with my Daniel responsibilities, that left us plenty of time for fun. And at least some of our fun involved tormenting Jacob.

Jacob had dirty blond hair, serious brown eyes, and a quiet demeanor like Mom, and it was no secret that he was her favorite. She doted on him and declared nearly every morning at scripture reading that she was raising a future Mormon prophet.

"You're my little Nephi," she would coo to Jacob as she cradled him in her arms. Nephi was an ancient prophet we read about in *The Book of Mormon*. Sometimes Mom jokingly referred to Connie and me as Laman and Lemuel, Nephi's evil older brothers.

Mom had Jacob on such a pedestal that Heidi and I decided he needed to be put in his place.

Sometimes, we would convince him to stand on the front porch while we threw darts at him. Other times, we blended together ice cubes with the most disgusting mix of ingredients we could hunt down—tomatoes, eggs, Tabasco sauce, salt, and peanut butter—and served them to him as shakes. "I know what we could do," Heidi said once when we were bored. "Let's invite Ernie over for a playdate. That will really tick off Jacob."

Ernie lived down the street and was the one kid that we knew Jacob couldn't stand. We both doubled over in laughing fits just thinking about the look on Jacob's face when Ernie showed up at the door.

Heidi flipped through our church phone directory and found his family's last name. Then I made the call.

"Well, hi, Ernie," I spoke sweetly into the phone. "Jacob has been begging for a playdate with you the entire morning. Do you think you could come over and hang out this afternoon?"

We didn't tell Jacob about his pending playdate until Ernie knocked on the door. Jacob didn't say anything. But he was so angry he balled his hands into fists, and I thought he was going to hit us.

When we weren't pulling pranks on Jacob, I could count on Heidi for other entertainment ideas. Unlike Connie and me, who both had auburn-brown hair and brown eyes, Heidi was the spitting image of Dad. She had strawberry-blond hair and blue-green eyes, and a temper every bit as fiery as his. She also had his manipulation abilities.

During the school year, I usually hung out with my friend, Phyllis. She was a Navajo Indian who came up from a reservation in New Mexico each school year as part of the Mormon's Indian Student Placement Program. But she always went back to the reservation during the summer, and with her gone and Connie at work, Heidi and I quickly forged a bond.

Along with spending all of our time together during the week while Mom was at work, the two of us started hanging out on weekends.

Now that Mom had regular money coming in from the Health Department, a lot of her stress disappeared and she was less strict. On Saturdays, after our chores were done, she let

Heidi and me spend entire afternoons walking the three-mile stretch to the Cache Valley Mall to spend the hard-earned money I had accumulated during the week.

And on Sunday afternoons after church, she allowed us to walk around the neighborhood visiting elderly widows from the ward—whom we referred to as "sisters."

It was Heidi's idea. Mom had once made us visit a few of the widows in the ward as part of a fellowship effort, and they'd been so happy to have guests that they'd given us cookies and chocolates.

"Just think it about it," Heidi said in her "we'd be crazy not to do it" tone. "It's a way to get out of the house and get dessert."

One Sunday afternoon, we picked three of our favorite widows and began making the rounds. Heidi knocked on the door, but I always did the talking.

"Well, hi there, Sister Williams," I would say in the kindest voice I could conjure. "We were just thinking about you and wanted to drop by and say hello."

We could count on the response.

"Well, aren't you two just the sweetest angels. Why don't you come in and visit for a while? Are you thirsty or hungry?"

"Well, we had lunch but we could always go for a dessert," Heidi would say quickly. "But we can't stay long and don't want to be any trouble."

"Oh, you girls are no trouble. You just sit right down and relax, and I'll be right back."

Heidi would always shoot me a sly smile as we sank into the afghan-covered sofa and waited for our snacks.

"See," Heidi would say as soon as we got out the door,

sometimes packing a loaf of banana bread or a plate of chocolate chip cookies the sister had insisted we take with us. "Isn't this a lot better than hanging around at the house listening to Mom's Tabernacle Choir music?"

Dad stopped by for a one-day visit sometime in September and then didn't come home again until Christmas. Soon after he left, Mom started talking about divorce.

Mom had mentioned the possibility of divorce before, but now that things were going so well with her Health Department job, she brought it up a lot—like she was trying to get up the guts to do it.

"Part of it would be for protection," Mom told Connie and me after dinner once. "Your dad has bad credit and I don't want to lose the house."

Mom already had permission from Bishop Jones, who couldn't stand Dad and told her it was time to move on with her life. She asked Connie, who was almost fifteen and sometimes acted as her advisor, what she should do.

"I think you should do whatever you want to do," Connie replied with her trademark eye roll. "I don't know what difference it's going to make, do you?"

Like Connie, I didn't have a strong feeling either way. I still loved Dad as much as ever and waited by the phone when we were expecting his call. But he had only been home a couple of times since Daniel had been born and my life had changed a lot since then.

Though Mom hired a babysitter for Daniel when I started

sixth grade, I was still in charge after school because Connie played sports and Mom didn't get home until nearly six. Between watching over Heidi and Jacob, doing homework, and working through my list of daily chores, I didn't have much time to think about Dad.

I had given up on the idea of escape. In my twelve-year-old mind, I couldn't imagine how divorce would change anything.

After months of talking about it, Mom went to see a lawyer, and when Dad dropped by again on the Saturday before Easter, she greeted him with divorce papers.

"What in the hell is this?" he yelled before storming back out of the house.

The next day, he and Mom locked themselves in their bedroom and stayed there for what felt like hours. Connie and I waited in the kitchen, anxious to know what was happening.

When the bedroom door finally opened, Dad came out and shut the door behind him, leaving Mom inside. We watched him enter the hall and make a left turn into the living room. A minute later, his voice thundered for Connie to come to the living room.

Connie shot me a knowing look and headed for Dad.

I was so nervous my stomach was in knots, and the suspense was driving me crazy. I was dying to know what they were talking about, but I didn't dare make my way into the hallway in case Dad caught me eavesdropping.

I watched the second hand drag its way around the clock that hung on our kitchen wall. I wondered what Dad was saying to Connie and if Connie would let on that we already knew about the divorce. After five minutes that seemed to stretch into five hours, I saw her casually strolling toward me.

"It's your turn," she announced, her face blank.

I couldn't tell by looking at her how things had gone and I was too rattled to ask.

I raced down the hall, rounded the corner, and found Dad seated on the green woven couch the church had donated to us. He hated that couch because he viewed it as the bishop stepping into his business.

Dad looked different than I had ever seen him. His shoulders slumped forward and his face was pale. He didn't smile when I entered the room and his eyes were red, like he had been crying.

His appearance caught me off guard. I didn't expect him to be upset.

I took a seat next to him and leaned into him for a hug. He gave me a quick squeeze and then broke away. I sat in nervous silence, waiting for him to speak.

Dad stared straight ahead for what seemed like an hour. His hands were balled up into fists in his lap, not in an angry sort of way, more like he thought they would give him strength if he just clenched them hard enough.

His right fist was trembling.

I reached over and rested my hand on top of it until he opened his grip. Then I slid my hand into his and squeezed hard so he would know how much I loved him. This seemed to break Dad's trance. He looked over at me and his soft hazel gaze penetrated mine.

"Well, Ingrid," he said finally. "Your mother and I are getting a divorce."

Dad said it like he had just announced the world was coming to an end. His sadness surprised me. I didn't think he would care. He wasn't ever home anyway, and he and Mom fought so much when he was home that I thought it would be less stressful for everyone if they weren't married anymore.

I wanted to react appropriately to his mood, but since I had already known that the news was coming and hadn't really been bothered by it, I was having a hard time acting surprised or grief stricken. Still, it was upsetting to see him so sad.

I couldn't find the right words so I buried my head into his chest and hugged him hard.

"I love you, Dad," I said.

Dad let me hug him for a minute and then once again pulled away. Suddenly he was sitting upright and his face changed from sad to serious.

"Ingrid, I want to tell you something and I want you to listen to me real good. If you ever love another man or call another man 'Dad,' you won't be my daughter."

Dad's words stunned me. I looked at him to see if he was joking but his hazel eyes stared back at me hard.

I felt like I had been slapped. I was confused and my mind was racing. Why would I call another man "Dad"? I couldn't conceive of such a thing. Plus, that would mean that Mom would be married to someone else. I hadn't thought of that possibility.

I tried to digest this new bit of information, while focusing on what Dad had said about me loving another man or calling him "Dad."

"I could never love anyone else, Dad. And I would never call anyone else 'Dad.' You're my dad, no one else." I drew out my words and punctuated them to make it clear I was on his side, and that I was offended he had questioned my loyalty.

The tension between us melted as soon as I spoke. Dad smiled and hugged me, and then reached into his shirt pocket.

"I have something for you," he told me. He pulled out a gold bracelet with fake jade stones and fastened it around my wrist. I didn't know what to say. Dad had never given me a present before, not even on my birthday.

I lifted up my wrist to examine my new treasure. It was beautiful. The jade stones were oval and circled the entire bracelet. The bracelet made me feel special. I knew that Dad must really love me to give me something like this. But I also felt the weight of everything that was happening. Even though I hadn't expected anything to change, there was electricity in the air and I could feel things shifting.

I suddenly had the urge to cry and dove into Dad's arms for another hug. I buried my head into his chest and felt tears streaming down my cheeks. I felt safe and warm in his arms and didn't want to let go.

We embraced for a couple of minutes, but then I felt Dad gently pull away from me.

"Well, Ingrid, it's time for you to go now so I can tell the other kids what's happening," he said quietly. "But just remember how much I love you. And remember, you will always be my Hippie Boy."

7

. . .

It was like someone had waved a magic wand over Dad and turned him into the parent I had wished for my whole life.

A few days after our divorce talk, he stopped by the house for a surprise visit.

"Well, kids, I've decided to move to Salt Lake City. I'm starting a tool business there. This way, we can see a lot more of each other."

His grin lit up his entire face and his eyes twinkled. All of the sadness was gone. He was back to being himself—only better.

Even Connie, who never showed much emotion, let out a whoop of joy. I considered pinching myself to make sure it was real. I charged into Dad's open arms for a hug.

"This is so great, Dad," I gushed. "It's the best news ever."

Salt Lake City was just a ninety-minute car ride away, but it seemed like another world. I had been there only a few times in my life, mainly to go to General Conference, a twice annual event held by the Mormon prophet and his twelve apostles. We never actually got to go into the Tabernacle, the large gathering hall where the event took place, but Mom sometimes took us to hang out in Temple Square, the Mormon mecca that swallowed an entire city block in the heart of downtown. When we went, we would sit on the lawn outside of the Tabernacle and eat the egg salad sandwiches Mom had packed us while we listened to the prophet's sermon over loudspeakers.

Dad started dropping by the house at least once a week for a visit and often surprised us by taking us out to dinner at McDonald's.

My gut felt like it was going to burst with happiness. Dad was back in my life and I knew that I was now important to him. I had become his eyes and ears at the house, and he was counting on me to keep him informed.

Along with his official visits at the house, Dad and I started having secret visits. Sometimes when I walked the few blocks to my elementary school, I found him waiting for me at the corner.

"Well, how's my Hippie Boy doing?" he would ask, his arms open for a hug.

"Great," I would reply, throwing my arms around his neck and breathing in his Old Spice aftershave.

Then it was time to get down to business.

"What's going on in the house?" he would ask. "What's your Mom up to? Do you think your brothers and sisters still love me?"

I loved it that Dad now depended on me. He and I would walk slowly to my school while I recounted in detail all the happenings at home since his last visit.

"The kids are all doing fine, but they miss you a lot," I would start out, stretching the truth about the "missing him" part because I knew it was what Dad needed to hear. "Mom's just working a lot. And we had our scripture reading this morning as usual."

"Is she dating anyone yet?"

"No, but she's talking about going to some church dances when the divorce is final."

There was always a long pause after I mentioned Mom. The smile would leave Dad's face for a minute and the same sad look he wore when he told me about the divorce would appear. But then he would snap out of it and come back to me.

"Okay, you just keep me posted. Remember, you are my eyes and ears in that house."

Dad and I would part ways when we came to the school gate, but not before scheduling another secret meeting.

"Just remember that you are my Hippie Boy," he always whispered in my ear as he hugged me good-bye. "Don't ever let them tell you something different."

The "them" Dad referred to was Bishop Jones and his two counselors, whom Dad blamed for destroying his marriage to Mom and taking away his family. Dad told me that even though things had been rough between him and Mom, he had made a decision on his way home that Easter weekend to change his life and fix their marriage. He said his plan was to give up his life on the road and set up a business nearby, which is exactly what he was doing now in Salt Lake City with the tool business he was putting together.

"I really wanted to make things work, but that bishop convinced your mother I was no good and decided to destroy our family," Dad fumed. "He may think that he's holier than holy but I tell you what, Ingrid. He's going straight to hell."

When Dad shared his personal thoughts, it made me feel closer to him, and in my mind, I forgave him for all the times he was gone when I needed him, or for scaring us when he lost his temper. I could see how much Dad was hurting and needed me. It made me feel special.

When school let out for the summer, Dad invited all of us kids to Salt Lake City to stay with him at his new apartment for a few days. My brothers stayed behind with Mom, but Connie, Heidi, and I went. Dad still spent most of his time in business meetings, but he let us buy whatever food we wanted to eat at the grocery store, and even took us to Lagoon, a large amusement park near Salt Lake City.

At home things were better too. Mom smiled a lot and sometimes we caught her humming songs as she moved through the house. Her job at the Health Department was going so well she decided it was time to get a real car. She traded in our piece of junk Buick for an almost-new green and orange mini station wagon with wood paneling on the sides. It was clean inside and smelled like the tree-shaped alpine air freshener that hung from the rearview mirror.

I was proud of our new car. I was also proud of Mom. She had proven that she could support us and make it on her own just fine. She was even starting to be fun to be around.

Mom had always loved board games and puzzles, and we

began to spend several evenings a week gathered around the kitchen table playing Monopoly or working on one of the five hundred piece puzzles Mom picked up from the church thrift store. On Saturday nights, we all grabbed our pillows and headed to the living room for two hours of Mom's favorite shows: *The Love Boat* and *Fantasy Island*.

"Who wants to help me make the popcorn?" Mom would ask between commercials. "We need some snacks, don't we?"

"Maybe this divorce is what we needed to get our family back on track," I confided to Heidi during one of our now-regular weekend walks to the mall. "I mean, everyone is so much happier."

"Yeah, so far so good," she replied. "Let's just hope it lasts."

Like the summer before, I was in charge at home—earning my dollar-a-day wage. Connie, who had continued working weekends at the park during the school year, was back to the maximum thirty-two hours a week she was allowed to work as a fifteen-year-old minor.

For months, she had been saving up for a new ten-speed bike and a dog, and shortly after summer started, she was ready to buy both.

"Ingrid, I've got a surprise for you," Connie said one weekend, out of the blue. "How would you like my old ten-speed?"

I looked at her in shock. We didn't really hang out much anymore and I couldn't believe she was willing to just give me her bike when I knew she could probably sell it for fifty dollars.

"Are you kidding?" I blurted. "I would LOVE it! Thank you."

"Well, it's yours," she said simply. "Why don't you take it for a test drive so we can see if we need to adjust the seat?"

I would have hugged Connie but she didn't like people touching her. "Okay, got it. Thanks again," I called back to her, riding off on my new wheels.

Later that day, Connie brought home Abbey—the purebred Irish setter she had been dreaming of for months. She had found Abbey through a newspaper ad and decided to name her after a small Irish town she had read about.

"I even have papers to prove she's a purebred," Connie said proudly, pushing the document in front of me for proof.

"That's really cool, Connie."

I was still on such a high from getting the bike I would have told her anything she wanted to hear. But the truth is, I really did think it was cool. I wasn't into animals the way Connie was, but for a dog, I thought Abbey was beautiful. She had warm, chocolate eyes and a long, reddish-brown mane that was so smooth and soft it felt like silk. Mostly I loved the way the word "purebred" rolled off my tongue. Just saying it made me feel rich.

Mom's divorce from Dad became official in late June, and she immediately began going to the singles dances sponsored by the church. Now that Dad was around and Mom was happy, I didn't mind her going out; I thought it was good for her to start having a little fun.

Every Friday night, Mom made the transformation from weary working mother to single woman on the prowl. She spent an hour in front of the full-length mirror mounted to our bathroom door, curling her shoulder-length brown hair with Connie's curling iron, coloring in her blondish-brown eyebrows with a dark brown Avon eyebrow pencil, and carefully applying blue eye shadow. She would comb through her closet, looking for a skirt and blouse to wear, and then come back into the kitchen, where we all sat around the kitchen table watching her.

"Well, children, how do I look?" she would ask as she twirled in front of us.

Mom's clothes all came from the Deseret Industries, the church's version of the Goodwill, and she was drawn to dowdy skirts and floral printed blouses that looked like they belonged to the elderly sisters at church. Her petite five-foot-two frame was rounded out from five pregnancies, but I thought she had a pretty face and kind eyes. And though her thick Austrian accent made it hard to understand her at times, I figured some men would find it charming.

"You look great, Mom," Connie or I would reply. "You're going to knock 'em dead tonight."

Mom's happiness was infectious. It was fun watching her act like a teenager, and we could feel her excitement over the unknown future. Connie and I even started thinking it would be okay if she got remarried. Maybe she would meet someone really nice who would treat her like a queen and provide for her so she could stay at home and be a homemaker. And just maybe, Connie and I hoped, the guy would be rich and we would be able to move into a new house.

We always stayed up until Mom returned from her night out and quizzed her about her evening like nosy parents.

"So who did you dance with?" we asked as soon as she arrived. "What does he look like? Does he have kids? Does he have his own house? What part of town does he live in?"

Now that Mom was in the dating scene, we wanted to make sure she was dating the right kind of guy. It was important to us that he was nice, decent looking, and had something to offer. Our question about where he lived was a big indicator of what he brought to the table. If the guy lived on "the hill," chances were good that he lived in a nice house and was well-off financially. If he lived west of Main Street, on our side of town, he was likely to be poor.

Mom would laugh and then recount her stories from the evening. "First of all, the music was magical," she would say, settling onto the living room couch. "They played really beautiful songs like, 'Some Enchanted Evening.' And there were a few men who asked me to dance. They really weren't my type. One of them wore a cowboy hat, which I think is silly. But I just always say 'yes,' to dance with them once, and then thank them and return to my seat."

Given our hopes that she would meet a rich, intelligent, charming guy, Connie and I were disgusted when she started dating Karl, the only other divorced person we knew. Karl lived around the corner from us in a gloomy, one-bedroom basement apartment. He was a tall, lanky guy who was going bald and usually wore a blank, perplexed look on his face that made him seem like he had less brainpower than hair. He walked with his shoulders hunched forward and reminded me of a needy dog.

We nicknamed him Bert, after the *Sesame Street* character.

He was nice enough, but I couldn't stand the guy. He was a joke and I was embarrassed that Mom would stoop this low.

"It's nothing serious," Connie assured me in such a confident tone that I wondered if she had snuck a peek in Mom's journal. "She's just getting back into the swing of things."

8

. . .

By the time mid-August rolled around, I was counting down the days until school started. I was finally going to be in junior high and I couldn't wait.

Though Dad hadn't yet paid Mom the two hundred and fifty dollar monthly child support ordered by the court, he did give each of us kids seventy-five dollars for school clothes, which meant that for once I could start the school year with new clothes.

I was ecstatic.

To make sure our money stretched, Heidi and I spent days combing through the shops in the Cache Valley Mall searching for the best sales. I ended up with two new pairs of jeans, a couple of imitation IZOD shirts, and a copycat pair of Cherokee sandals, and I couldn't wait to show off my outfits.

I used some of the money I'd earned from my dollar-a-day babysitting job to pay for a "feathered" haircut and spent the week before school started perfecting my new hairdo by imitating Connie's moves with the curling iron.

"What you've got to do is put a big curl on each side of your forehead, then let the curl sit for five minutes so it holds better," Connie said, coaching me through the process. "Then you can brush it back—just make sure you spray it so it stays in place."

My best friend, Phyllis, was back from the reservation, and the first day of school, the two of us walked the halls like we owned them. Because she had been held back a year in second grade, Phyllis was a lot bigger and taller than I was. She was also more mature, and I felt safe and sophisticated with her by my side.

"This is going to be so much more fun than grade school, I guarantee you that," Phyllis declared as we pushed our way through the packed halls to our new lockers.

Though we didn't have any classes together, the two of us met up at lunch each day and by the end of our first week, we'd made plans to try out for the school volleyball team—one of the few extracurricular activities available to seventh graders.

It was Phyllis's idea.

"This way, we'll be able to hang out together," she said as we shoveled down the hamburgers now available to us from the school cafeteria. I was still receiving free lunches, but didn't mind because I could pick up my lunch tickets from the office each Monday morning so no one knew about it.

The tryouts were scheduled for 7:00 A.M. on the morning of September 11th. Mom offered to drive us and even agreed to get us there a half hour early so we had plenty of time to change and warm up.

It was barely 6 A.M. when we left our house to pick up Phyllis and the morning skies were still black. Phyllis lived on a farm in a rural part of town where there were no streetlights, and Mom flashed the car headlights three times to let her know we were waiting for her. Minutes later, she came running out to the car, her gym bag slung over her shoulder.

"How's it going?" she asked as she climbed into the backseat. "Are you ready for this? Think we'll both make the team?"

"Of course," I said, hoping that my sudden case of nerves wouldn't cause me to throw up my Cream of Wheat. I didn't want to admit it, but I knew Phyllis had a lot better shot at making the team than I did. For starters, she was tall.

Mom headed north on the rural road, aiming for the intersecting highway that would route us back into the center of town. There were no streetlights announcing the highway, only a stop sign. It was dark and Mom was having a difficult time seeing.

"We should be coming up on it at any time now," she said.

I felt the glare of bright lights through my window. I turned my head to see what it was. Then everything went black.

I awoke to sirens blasting through the shattered glass. The right side of my face felt hot and wet. A scream escaped from the backseat.

"Look at your face! It's covered in blood!" Phyllis was sobbing and I remembered that she was in the car with us. Her noise pounded against my head, which felt ready to explode.

I wanted to turn around to see what she was so upset about,

but I couldn't move. My right arm was pinned under a mass of metal. Large shards of glass covered my lap.

My head throbbed. I couldn't focus. For a minute, I thought I was having a bad dream. Then I heard moaning. I looked over at Mom, who was slumped back in her seat. I saw blood oozing from her head.

"We've been in a car accident," she mumbled. "Don't move." A jumble of voices and heavy footsteps erupted around us.

"Are you okay in there?" I heard. "Don't move. Your car door is crushed in around you and we're going to have to cut you out."

The sobs coming from Phyllis were getting louder. "Are you okay, Phyllis?" I mustered.

She didn't respond and I didn't have the energy to ask again. Two men were lifting Mom out of the car and onto a stretcher, and I heard someone help Phyllis out of the car. Then the men were at my door.

"Don't worry. We're going to get you out of there," a guy's voice said. "Everything's going to be fine."

A man reached through the broken window and put a brace around my neck. He said it was to keep my head stable and he told me I shouldn't try to move.

I closed my eyes and felt some sort of towel or cloth being pushed up against the right side of my face and head. A man's voice said something about trying to slow down the bleeding.

Then I heard the sound of metal cutting, and a few minutes later I was free. A sharp pain shot through my right shoulder.

"That hurts," I moaned.

"It's okay, honey," a voice said. "We're going to move you

real gently and then get you to the hospital so we can get you all fixed up."

I was lifted onto a stretcher and felt someone put gauze on my face and wrap my head. Then I was carried into the waiting ambulance. Out of my left eye, I saw Mom lying on a stretcher next to me. Her head was wrapped too.

"Where's Phyllis?"

"She's fine," Mom whispered over to me. "She's getting a ride to the hospital to be checked out, but everything's okay with her."

A few minutes later I was lying on a table in the emergency room with bright lights shining into my face. Several people gathered around me, cleaning up my face, giving me shots to deaden the pain. Then the doctor came and sewed up my face and head and covered them with bandages and gauze.

He x-rayed my right shoulder and neck and announced that my collarbone was broken. Someone pushed me forward while a nurse put a brace around my body and my right shoulder. When they finished, a couple of people lifted me onto a stretcher and a nurse wheeled me into a nearby corridor. I saw Mom lying on a stretcher across the hall.

"We just need to keep you here for a few minutes while we prepare a room for you and your mother," the nurse said softly.

I nodded. I didn't care where I was. I just wanted to sleep. I was drifting off when I heard Karl's voice.

"Ingrid," Mom called from across the hall. "Karl's going to give you a blessing."

Her words came at me like a shock of electricity. I was suddenly wide awake and felt a charge pumping through my body.

In the Mormon church, it was common for a priesthood-holding dad to bless his family members when they were sick or hurt. But Karl was not my dad or anything close to it, and there was no way I was going to let that goon touch me, let alone say some prayer over me.

I heard him coming toward me.

"Get away from me!" I yelled frantically. "Don't touch me!"

A surge of panic rushed through me. What was he even doing at the hospital? Where was Dad? Why wasn't Dad here?

"Ingrid, you stop that right this minute!" Mom barked from her stretcher.

Karl stepped behind me and rested his hands on my head. "Get AWAY from me!" I screamed. "Get AWAY!"

The nurse who had pushed my stretcher into the hallway a few minutes earlier came running.

"I don't know what's going on here but you are clearly upsetting her and you need to leave now!" she barked at Karl. As soon as she said it, his hands were gone and I heard his footsteps retreat.

I wanted to hug the nurse. "Thank you," I mumbled.

I could feel Mom's rage from across the hall. I didn't care. He was gone. I closed my eyes and drifted to sleep.

Later that morning, after the nurse had settled us into our room and left us so we could get some rest, Mom came unglued.

"Ingrid, you should be ashamed of yourself," she hissed from across the room. "I don't know who you think you are, but Karl is a good man and he deserves some respect. The next time you see him, you had better apologize."

Tears streamed down the layer of gauze and bandages that

covered my swollen face. My head and face throbbed, and my body was stiff and sore. Every time I tried to shift positions to get comfortable, pain shot through my right shoulder and collarbone. I was miserable but Mom didn't bother asking me how I was doing. All she cared about was her new boyfriend.

I pretended I didn't hear her. I closed my eyes and acted like I was sleeping. I ignored her as much as possible for the rest of the day and was relieved when the doctor checked in on us early the next morning and announced that Mom could go home.

"You'll have to keep an eye on that concussion and go easy on those fractured ribs," I heard the doctor tell Mom. "But it's nothing a little rest won't fix."

Karl came to get Mom an hour later. Finally, I could relax.

I spent the morning watching TV and being attended to by nurses. They brought me grilled chicken, mashed potatoes and chocolate cake from the hospital cafeteria and stopped in every hour or so to see if I needed anything.

Early that afternoon, Dad came.

He entered the room carrying the most beautiful flower arrangement I had ever seen. It featured a ceramic girl with soft blue eyes and a brown bonnet on her head. In her arms, she held a colorful bouquet of fresh daisies and tulips.

My heart danced. Dad hadn't forgotten me. "Hi, Dad," I called across the room.

"How's my beautiful girl?" he replied.

Dad walked over to a table near my bed and set down the flower arrangement. Then he knelt beside me and took my hand in his.

"How are you, sweetheart? Are you doing okay?"

I nodded. His hands were shaking and I noticed that his eyes were red. "No one called me to tell me what happened, Ingrid," he said. "Can you believe it? No one bothered to tell me you had been in a car accident. I didn't find out until your grandma called me this morning." Then his eyes settled on the bandages that covered my face.

"What happened to my beautiful girl?" he said, shaking his head sadly. Dad stayed with me for about an hour and then left, promising me that he would stay in close touch.

I enjoyed my break in the hospital and spent the next day relaxing. None of my brothers and sisters came to visit, which was fine with me. But just before dinner, my young women's class from church came and brought flowers. They formed a line and took turns stopping by my bed. Most of them just asked me how I was feeling and told me they hoped I would get better soon. But when Theresa, one of the prettiest girls in my class, got to me, she covered her mouth and let out a little scream.

Later that evening, a nurse took off the bandages to check on my stitches and told me she was going to leave them off so the wounds could breathe. Afterward, she helped me to the bathroom.

When I saw my face in the mirror, I screamed too.

The right side of my forehead was purple, green, and lumpy, and covered in a mass of black stitches. Another thick, jagged row of black stitches stretched from my lip up through the middle of my right cheek. I looked like a monster.

I cried myself to sleep that night and didn't fight it when Mom stopped by the next day with a couple of elders I liked from church and asked if they could give me a blessing.

They put some ointment on my head and then placed their hands over it and started praying. When they got to the part about my face healing so I would look beautiful, I closed my eyes and added my own silent prayer.

After a few days in the hospital, I was released and sent home to recover. The hope and happiness of the past few months were gone, and the air in the house was once again suffocating and dark.

I spent a week propped up on a church-donated armchair in the living room, too discouraged to even change out of my bathrobe. The right side of my face and forehead was a mass of wiry black stitches and bluish, purple lumps. My right shoulder was still pinned to my body with a brace designed to hold my collarbone in place until the fracture could heal, and I hurt everywhere—inside and out.

Mom was also sad again. And our almost new mini station wagon was totaled, replaced by a rusted white Chevy Impala Mom had found.

I was relieved that Karl stopped coming around. But now Mom's Friday night trips to the singles dances took on an air of desperation. The fun and sparkle disappeared from her eyes, and Connie and I stopped waiting up to ask her how her evening had gone.

Mom spent a couple of weeks dating a twenty-eight-year-old guy named Mike but broke it off when she found out he had once taken drugs.

Then she met Earl.

Years later, I asked her why she agreed to marry him even though they had only dated for a month—especially when she knew that all of us kids were so against it.

She was quiet for a minute.

"I wanted someone to lead me," she said finally. "I guess I didn't want to have to make the decisions anymore.

"It all would have worked out fine if he had been a righteous leader," she added.

9

. . .

A.E. (After Earl): Spring 1980

After Earl forbade me to go on the weekend trip to New Mexico with Dad, a line was drawn, and Mom landed squarely on Earl's side. As far as I was concerned, she was now the enemy.

Their wedding reception, like most Mormon wedding receptions, was held in the church gym immediately following their temple marriage. Mom ordered all of us kids to put on our best Sunday clothes and come to the gym to join in their celebration. And once we were there, she insisted on having a family picture taken with Earl.

The idea of having any association with that greasy-haired creep made my blood boil. Earl wore a powder-blue tuxedo that blended with his pasty pale skin. He had removed his glasses for the picture but his eyes still looked like they were going to pop out of his head. And there was no escaping his cold, icy-blue stare.

"But he's not part of our family," I seethed, fighting the urge to bolt out of the building.

"Ingrid, get in this picture right now!" Mom barked. Connie and I glared at her and then at the photographer. We took our spots in the back on the far left of Earl, trying to secure as much distance as possible between us and him. In the picture, I stared straight ahead—the hatred oozing from my eyes.

The next day, Mom and Earl left for their honeymoon, but not before arranging for Brother Hammond, a good friend to Mom and a priesthood holder from church, to stay with us. I overheard him and Mom talking about the need for an adult to be there in case Dad "tried to do something crazy." Dad hadn't come around since the incident with Earl and I knew his rage was as intense as mine because he had called me a week after to talk about it. "If I hadn't gotten out of there when I did, I would have killed that son of a bitch," Dad said, his voice rising.

"What I want to know is why you stayed around and didn't stand up to them," he continued. "Why didn't you just tell them you were going with me to New Mexico anyway?

"Let me tell you something, Ingrid. No one has the right to keep you from your daddy. The next time that happens, there's only one thing to do. You tell them to go to hell and you come with me."

"Okay, I will," I said quietly, my face flushed with anger. I wanted to scream into the phone, ask him why he didn't stand up for me. Why he just stormed out of the house and left me there. Instead, I told him I loved him and hung up the phone.

Mom and Earl spent nearly a week exploring the national parks in Southern Utah. But instead of returning home happy and refreshed, Mom looked tired and defeated. Her steps were heavy, like she was carrying a hundred-pound weight on her back, and her eyes looked even sadder than before.

The next morning at scripture reading, she told us it was time to set some new ground rules.

"Earl and I have talked and we feel that you children should call him something that shows respect," she said. "We know the name 'Dad' is reserved for your dad, and is special to you. So we would like you to call Earl 'Father.'"

I looked at Earl, who was seated next to Mom on the couch. He was staring at me and flashed the same mean smile he wore when he announced that God didn't want me spending time with my dad.

I shifted my gaze to Mom, who stared at the ground, pretending like what she had just asked us to do was as normal as asking someone to pass the butter.

I shot an imploring look at Connie, who appeared ready to blow.

I looked back at Mom, wondering what happened to her promise that Earl wouldn't try to take the place of Dad.

"But he's not our father," I said, punctuating my words to get my point across.

"I can tell you one thing right now," Connie fumed. "I am not calling him that."

"I'm not either," Heidi added.

Jacob and Daniel, now eight and two, said nothing.

"This isn't respectful!" Earl bellowed at Mom. "Tell your kids to show me some respect!"

"Why don't you start showing us some respect?" Connie snarled back. Mom looked like a deer caught in headlights.

"Children, stop this right now!"

A long minute of silence followed.

Mom glared at us and then turned to Earl. "Why don't we start scriptures? We'll talk about this again later," she said softly.

I had ten weeks to go until summer break and survived each day by crossing it off on the calendar that hung on my bedroom wall, counting down the days until school was out and I could be with Dad. He had invited me and my sisters to stay with him for a while during the summer, and Mom, who was already exhausted by the war now raging in our house, readily agreed to let us go.

The atmosphere at home was tense and hostile. It started at 6 A.M., when Mom summoned us out of bed for our morning scriptures. Earl now lorded over the green couch, causing Connie, Heidi, and me to retreat to a spot on the floor at the far end of the room so we could steer clear of him and his smell.

There was a new pecking order in our house: Earl, then the rest of us. Shortly after moving in, he announced that as the priesthood holder and man, he was the head of the household and was now in charge. At morning scripture time, Earl now decided who would read from the scriptures and what scriptures to read. He chose the hymns we sung and he said the closing prayer—unless he decided Mom or one of us kids should say it, at which point we were supposed to follow his command immediately and launch into prayer.

Earl never lifted a hand to help clean the house or make the food. He said that was a woman's job. He also didn't like the meals we ate as a family. He wanted meat. Mom, always in a hurry to get out the door to work in the morning and always exhausted from her day, became his indentured servant. In the morning, she piled Earl's plate with bacon and sausage while the rest of us ate our Cream of Wheat cereal. At night, she loaded up his plate with the buffalo meat and venison he had stuffed into our deep freezer when he moved in.

Breakfast wasn't bad because everyone was in a hurry to get out the door and we ate in relative peace. But dinner was a nightmare.

Earl sat at one end of our long, rectangular plastic banquet table. He had declared that spot the "head of the table" and the place where the "head of the family" should sit. Every evening he took his seat and waited for the separate meal he'd ordered Mom to make to be placed in front of him.

Earl had implemented a "no talking unless spoken to" rule and was the only one who could initiate the conversation. Other than reading scriptures or praying, our family rarely interacted with each other anyway, so aside from being annoyed that he had made the rule, I didn't care about not talking; it meant I could zone out and shut out his sound and smells. What pissed me off was when he addressed me and actually expected me to respond. Connie and Heidi felt the same way. As a result, sitting down for dinner was like sitting on top of an active volcano.

Like most dinners, we spent the Tuesday evening after Easter sitting around the table, staring silently at the plate of food in front of us while we waited for Earl to bless it.

He took his time looking around the table to make sure everyone had their arms folded before he started.

"Our Father, bless this food that my wife prepared for me and that we are about to eat. And bless this family that they will listen to my guidance and the authority you have given me as the priesthood holder and rightful head of this household."

It was everything I could do not to scream and start punching in walls. I opened my eyes and looked across the table at Connie, who was staring blankly at the wall in front of her.

Earl finished his prayer with a loud "Amen" and Mom repeated it. The rest of us grabbed our forks and started concentrating on the Hamburger Helper Mom had made for us, trying to shut out the sounds of Earl attacking the slab of undercooked venison heaped on his plate.

Earl cleared his throat. "Connie, how was your day today?" he started, his tone demanding and condescending.

Mom may have been buying this whole priesthood authority crap but Connie wasn't about to play into his game. She ignored him and continued eating her food.

Earl was prepared for this because it was a repeat of almost every other dinner. He leaned over his venison-filled plate so his face was within inches of Connie's.

"Connie! I asked you how your day was and you are going to answer me!"

She stayed silent, which I knew took some serious willpower with Earl polluting her airspace with his rotten-hamburger breath. I bit my lip to suppress a laugh. Connie had just turned sixteen and had decided she didn't have to take this crap from Earl. In her defiance, I felt like she was standing up for all of us, and I was proud of her for sticking to her resolve.

Mom, fearing a fight, spoke up.

"Connie, Earl asked you a question. Please answer him."

Connie looked up from her plate at Mom and saw the pleading look on her face. She slowly turned toward Earl and glared at him for a long minute.

"FINE!" she said with such force that I could see spit flying out of her mouth.

"WHAT did you just say to me?" Earl bellowed, shaking his meat-filled fork in Connie's face. "If you think you can get away with talking to me like that, you are wrong!"

Connie looked back down at her plate and resumed eating. Earl turned his anger on Mom.

"Tell your daughter to show me some respect! I'm warning you, do it NOW!"

Mom's face wore a mix of fear and resignation.

"Connie, Earl asked you a question. Please answer him."

"I did! I said my day was fine!"

Earl jumped up from his head-of-the-household seat.

"That's not good enough! You need to show me some respect! When I ask you how your day is, I expect you to tell me. And I don't mean a one-word answer!"

By now, I had lost any appetite I had for the hamburger-noodle mixture on my plate. I just wanted to be away from this. I glanced at Heidi, who kept her eyes focused on her plate. I noticed that Jacob had pushed his chair closer to Mom. Daniel was now on Mom's lap and was burying his face into her shoulder.

"I don't need to put up with this!" Connie screamed, shoving her chair away from the table. "I'm out of here!"

She stormed out of the kitchen, ran down the hall, and slammed the front door behind her.

My heart was pounding. I had to get out of there too. I pushed my chair back from the table and picked up my plate to take it to the sink.

"Where do you think you're going?" Earl spewed. "I didn't excuse you from the table! Sit down right now!"

"NO! You're not the boss of me! Don't tell me what to do!"

Mom jumped in, determined to regain some control of the situation. "Ingrid, you sit down at that table right this minute!"

Sometimes at this point in the dinner fight, I had the courage to follow Connie out the door or run to my attic room and barricade myself inside, but something about Mom's voice made me stay put.

I sank back into my chair and felt my fingers curling into fists as I listened to Earl's repeated demands that Mom do something to make us respect him before he took matters into his own hands.

I was scared that he would turn his anger on me. But after a few minutes he wore himself out, pushed away from the table, and headed for the living room. Mom followed behind him.

That was the sign for all of us that it was safe to leave the table. I cleared the dishes and began washing them, wishing I was anywhere else.

Though Mom was determined to fulfill her "devoted Mormon wife" role and seemed resigned to her new second-class citizen status, the one area in which she stood firm was in the baby department. She felt that it was both her duty and right to bring as many spirit children into the world as possible and she was determined to have at least one child with Earl. There was only one problem: Earl had gotten a vasectomy, and he had lied to Mom about it.

Years later, Mom told me that prior to getting married, Earl had told her he wanted more children as much as she did and had promised that they would start trying right away. It was one of the reasons Mom—who was then forty years old and worried she was running out of time—had hurried into the marriage. Earl waited until they were on their honeymoon to tell her about the vasectomy.

"That's when I knew I had made a huge mistake," Mom told me. "He started acting different and showing his true colors the minute we got married. But what could I do? I couldn't just tell the bishop that I wanted to get another temple divorce."

Mom was so angry about the betrayal that Earl reluctantly agreed to a vasectomy-reversal operation. For a week afterward, he laid sprawled out on the green couch in his powder blue cotton pajamas, polluting the living room with his rotten hamburger stench while whining that he was too sore to move. When he did get up to go to the bathroom, he walked as though a two-by-four had been wedged between his legs.

The thought of Mom actually having a baby with Earl was so repulsive to me that I started begging God not to let it happen. This time, our lack of money didn't even factor into my panic. That was nothing compared to the horror of having a half sibling that carried his genes.

A few weeks before school let out, Dad called to say he had a girlfriend. "I think you are really going to like her, Ingrid. Rhonda's a good person and she lets people do their own thing. She's not addicted to religion and she doesn't try to rule anybody.

"And she sure as hell isn't looking to be a mother to anyone else," he added with a laugh. "She has three daughters of her own, and believe me, that's more than enough."

Dad's news didn't even faze me. In fact, I was kind of happy about it. I hoped Mom would get jealous and realize what a horrible mistake she had made.

So that we could meet Rhonda, Dad invited Connie, Heidi, and me to spend the weekend with him in Salt Lake City. But instead of going to his apartment, he surprised us by renting a room at the Holiday Inn Fun Center.

"I figure you girls deserved a little break from Earl," Dad said. "So I thought we'd do something special this weekend."

It was like entering an amusement park. The hotel had an indoor swimming pool and hot tub, a miniature golf course, two Ping-Pong tables, and an arcade.

Dad reached into his pocket and pulled out a roll of quarters for each of us. "Here, this ought to cover you for a while. Don't spend it all at once because it's got to last you."

Dad spent the day in the hotel room making business calls while my sisters and I alternated between the swimming pool, the miniature golf course, and the game room.

At around six that evening, Dad ordered pizza and Rhonda arrived with her daughter Andrea and Andrea's baby son, Jackson. Natalie and Dana, Rhonda's other two daughters, weren't with her.

I knew from Dad that Natalie, who was thirteen like me, was a party girl who was always staying out late and getting into trouble. I was intimidated and even a little envious when I heard this because it sounded like she was much more sophisticated than I was. Dad said Dana was nineteen, worked at a record shop, and spent most of her time with her boyfriend.

I took in Andrea first. Dad had told me that she was sixteen, and though Mom made me skip our sex education class at school so I wouldn't get any ideas, I had discussed the topic enough with my friends to know how babies were made.

I liked it that Andrea had a baby. I thought it made her cool and mature. Andrea was beautiful. She had long, dark hair, sea-blue eyes, and smooth, flawless olive skin. She wasn't much taller than me, only five foot three or five foot four, but I thought she was movie star material. Just looking at Andrea made me feel self-conscious. Though my scar had faded some since the car accident, a thick layer of scar tissue ran from the corner of my mouth to halfway up my right cheek, and I knew it was the first thing anybody noticed about me. I had also recently hit puberty and gained ten pounds. Next to her, I felt fat and ugly.

At ten, I figured Heidi probably didn't care much about looks. But I wondered what Connie was thinking. She was the same age as Andrea and definitely had more of a sporty look about her now. She and Andrea were about as opposite as two people could get.

"Hi," I said awkwardly. "Nice to meet you. Cute baby."

"Thanks," Andrea said.

I turned my attention to Rhonda. For a mother, I thought she was attractive—and she was definitely a lot more modern looking than Mom. Rhonda had reddish-brown hair that she wore in a short, layered cut that had been teased with a comb and sprayed in place so that it couldn't move. She was thin and was made up with purple eye shadow, a thick coat of mascara, and a layer of foundation. I liked her smile, and her green eyes looked kind, but she seemed very nervous and her hands shook the whole time we were eating pizza. Later, I found out that she smoked—something Dad couldn't stand.

We didn't say much to each other. We just all smiled awkwardly and ate our pizza. After a couple of hours, they left.

Though I was a little worried about how Rhonda and her daughters would accept me, I liked it that Dad had a new girlfriend. I was proud that she was pretty and relieved that she wasn't religious. Dad wasn't settling for some loser like Mom had.

As soon as school let out, Dad picked up my sisters and me and took us to the new double-wide trailer he had recently rented in a suburb south of Salt Lake City. The minute we pulled into the neatly kept trailer park and I spied the swimming pool, I knew

I was going to have a good summer. Dad's trailer was spotless and smelled new.

I thought it was beautiful.

Like our Mississippi house, Dad's double-wide trailer was covered in wall-to-wall, short-shag, cream carpet. The door opened into a small living room, with an island counter that separated it from the kitchen. The trailer had two bedrooms, one where my sisters and I slept, and the master bedroom where Dad slept. Dad's bedroom had a large bathroom with a round Jacuzzi tub and a walk-in closet packed with suits. We instinctively felt his room was off-limits, but once, when he was at his office, Connie and I snuck into his closet and began counting his clothes. Connie started on one end and counted suits. I took on the dress shirts.

Connie finished first.

"He's got thirty-one of them!" she announced, her voice a mixture of amazement and disgust. "Can you believe it? Thirty-one! He could wear one every day of the month and never run out."

I counted more than a hundred dress shirts, most of them white. It was like entering a men's clothing store. Many of the suits were still in their bags and looked as though they hadn't even been worn. The ones not in suit bags smelled like Old Spice aftershave. I buried my face into one of the jacket sleeves and inhaled. I loved Dad's smell.

Connie was upset by all of Dad's clothes, given the hand-me-downs and secondhand store clothes we were usually forced to wear. But I was proud of Dad and his fancy wardrobe. To me, it was proof that he was starting to become a successful businessman. I knew that presidents of companies had to look nice.

Sometimes the three of us would go swimming at the trailer park swimming pool. Most of the time, though, we accompanied Dad to his office. JB Systems, Dad's tool business, was housed in a large warehouse located in a business park a few miles from his trailer. Aside from the restroom, the building consisted of a single ten-thousand-square-foot room that was divided in half by a wall of Sheetrock. The back section, which could only be accessed from the outside by two floor-to-ceiling steel garage doors, housed the tools—everything from screwdrivers, hammers, and wrenches, to metric socket sets and power drills. When Dad's sales crew was ready to hit the road, they just backed up their trucks to the loading dock, opened up the garage doors, and loaded up the tools.

The front half of the warehouse was an empty, open space that Dad envisioned would one day be filled with cubicles and office workers. His desk sat in the left front corner and faced the only window, which looked out onto the warehouse parking lot. Dad spent most of his day there, pacing in front of his desk as he talked on the phone with his sales guys, his tool suppliers, and the numerous people to whom he owed money.

I was mesmerized by Dad and could spend hours just sitting in a metal chair next to his desk, listening to him talk business. I loved the rhythm of his voice and felt so happy just to be in his presence that it didn't matter what I was doing. With Dad, there were no rules. We didn't have to read scriptures in the morning, didn't have to go to church on Sundays, and didn't have to deal with Earl. We also didn't have to do much housecleaning because Dad was rarely at his trailer and we usually ate our meals at McDonald's or Denny's.

Connie and Heidi didn't find life with Dad nearly as appealing. They were bored and Connie needed to go back home anyway because she was starting her summer park job again. Within a week, they both left. I knew Dad had hoped they would stay longer. But I was secretly happy they were gone because it meant that I had both the bedroom and Dad to myself.

The two of us quickly fell into a daily routine. We both prided ourselves on being early birds and each day we got up at 6 A.M., showered, dressed, and headed to Denny's for a quick breakfast. Then we drove to the office, where I entertained myself for the next several hours while Dad talked on the phone. When Dad needed to go to the bank or the post office, I tagged along. When he needed a Sugar Free Dr Pepper, I ran to the office park vending machines and bought one for both of us.

Dad's tool business was thriving. His sales crew was selling so many tools that he purchased two semitrucks and had the words "JB Systems" painted on the side of each. Dad had always said he was going to be a millionaire, and with his business growing the way it was, I was sure it was now only a matter of time.

"You want me to let you in on a little secret?" he asked me one day as were driving home from the office.

"Yeah, of course," I answered, thrilled that Dad wanted to confide in me.

A mischievous smile spread across his face. "It's about how I got started in this tool business."

Dad told me that after Mom served him with divorce papers,

he was devastated and rented a cheap motel room for a few days while he figured out what to do. He said he wanted to come off the road so he could spend more time with us kids, but he didn't have the money to rent an apartment and establish himself in business.

"I didn't know what to do but I needed cash to pay my motel bill, so I headed to the bank to withdraw the two hundred dollars I had in my checking account. But when I got there, I discovered the bank had made a mistake and had credited seven thousand dollars in canceled checks to my account."

Dad paused for effect and I laughed with excitement.

"I tell you what, Ingrid. It was like manna from heaven. I decided to hurry and empty the account before the bank discovered its mistake. Just like that, my problem was solved. With seven thousand dollars, I had enough money to set up my tool business.

"You see, Ingrid. You never know when opportunity will come your way. The way I view it, it was a short-term loan from the bank."

Dad told me he used the money to rent the apartment he had started off in and office space. Then he went to a local tool wholesaler and stocked up on inventory. Next, he gave each of the guys who worked on the road with him a few hundred dollars' worth of tools on consignment. When they ran out of tools, Dad shipped more out to them. Within a month, business was booming.

"I knew at some point the bank would figure it out and about a month ago, I received a call from the bank president," Dad continued. "He said he wanted to meet. I tell you what, Ingrid,

I was nervous. I mean, can you imagine what I was feeling? But I went to that meeting acting innocent, like I had no idea what he wanted to discuss."

"So what did you do? What happened?"

Dad chuckled. "Oh, you should have seen him, Ingrid. He was so angry he was shaking. He said, 'Mr. Ricks, do you mean to tell me you didn't know that the money wasn't yours?' I looked him straight in the eye and I said, 'Sir, do you mean to tell me that your bank doesn't know how much money is in people's accounts?' We both just stared at each other for a minute. Then he told me he wanted the money back and I told him that if a mistake had been made, I would be happy to pay it back, but I said that I could only do it in installments. In the end, we agreed to payback terms of a few hundred dollars a month.

"So you see, Ingrid, it all worked out just fine."

He laughed again and then got serious. "I want you to remember something about your daddy. I'm a creative financier. I don't do things the traditional way. But I always figure out how to make things work."

I shifted closer to Dad and gave him a hug. I was proud that he was able to talk his way out of trouble and leave even the president of a bank at a loss for words. Dad was special that way. He could talk his way out of anything.

The freedom I had with Dad was intoxicating. He told me he believed in treating me like an adult, not a child, and he talked to me like I was his equal, always asking for my opinion and always listening to my point of view. He trusted me and let me do whatever I wanted to do. In return, I danced circles to please him. I washed and dried our laundry at the trailer park Laundromat each week, and made sure that the trailer stayed spotless. Whenever Dad needed to get a tool shipment out to one of his sales guys, I helped box up the merchandise and label it.

Life was easy. Most evenings we kicked back at the trailer and watched TV, relaxing in comfortable silence. Now that it was just the two of us, we started buying TV dinners for our evening meals, which I prepared for us in the microwave. On weekend nights, Dad usually headed out on a date with Rhonda. I loved my alone time. I spent the time reading or flipping through the stack of fashion magazines Dad bought for me. Sometimes, I took long baths in his Jacuzzi tub. I felt relaxed and calm.

Aside from Dad's desk and a few chairs, the one other piece of furniture in the office was a mini jogger trampoline that Dad had picked up, thinking it would be a great way for him to get in a little exercise during the day. I often passed my time at the office jumping on it and decided that I was going to get serious and drop a few pounds.

Just before seventh grade ended, our gym teacher had made us line up in single file to be weighed. One by one, she motioned for us to step onto the scale. When it was my turn, she called out the words "One hundred and three pounds!" in a voice I was sure was loud enough for everyone to hear. I was so ashamed I wanted to burst into tears. I was only five foot one and had started to feel fat even before Mrs. Shipley confirmed it for me. But at home, Mom insisted that I eat everything on my plate, which made losing weight impossible.

That night after dinner, I locked myself in the bathroom and stuck my finger down my throat to make myself throw up like the anorexic girl I had read about in the book, *The Best Little Girl in the World*. But it backfired miserably. I hated the sensation of throwing up and when I finally triggered the vomit, it didn't just come out of my throat, it came shooting out my nose. I couldn't breathe and started gagging and gasping for air, which is when I heard pounding on the bathroom door.

"Ingrid, what's going on in there?" Mom demanded, her voice sounding more angry than concerned. "Open the door right this minute!"

The vomit was still flying out of my nose, spraying the toilet seat and the floor around it, and chunks of dinner were pushing their way up my throat. I couldn't leave the toilet, and answering her was out of the question.

"Ingrid, I'm serious. Open the door. Now!"

I waited at the toilet until my stomach had emptied itself and then crawled over to the door and turned the lock. My throat and nostrils were burning and I noticed that some of the vomit had ended up in my hair.

Mom came barging in, took one look at me, and shook her head in disgust.

"What were you doing in here?" she asked sharply. "Did you do this to yourself?"

I was too sick to invent a story. I nodded my head.

"Well, I hope you learned your lesson," she said, fuming. Then she turned around and stomped out of the room.

I concluded while washing the floor that I'd rather be fat than go through that experience again, but now that I had a chance to lose weight without having to throw up after each meal, I decided to go for it. I stopped by a drugstore and found a calorie counting book, and then told Dad I wanted to start bringing my lunches to the office. For the rest of June and the month of July, I lived on iceberg lettuce and boiled eggs. I skipped breakfast each morning and when I did accompany Dad to McDonald's, I limited my order to a kid's size hamburger, and then forced myself to chew each bite fifteen times before swallowing. At night, I dressed up my iceberg lettuce and eggs with two slices of bacon that I crumbled on top of it.

"You're something else, you know that, Ingrid?" Dad said watching me one evening, shaking his head. "With that determination of yours, you'll be able to do anything you want in life. And if what you want right now is to lose weight, I'm going to do everything in my power to support you."

The next day, Dad took me to a bookstore and gave me money to buy a Jane Fonda exercise video. I started doing aerobics at the trailer for an hour every evening. Sometimes Dad even joined me. And while he talked on the phone at the office, I alternated between sit-ups, jumping jacks, and jogging on the mini trampoline.

By the time I returned home in August, I was down to eighty-eight pounds. Dad had bought me several new pairs of shorts because my old ones were now too big. I felt fantastic.

"How did you do it?" Connie asked. I could hear the jealousy in her voice.

"Oh, I just went on a diet and did a little exercise," I answered casually. Mom didn't notice my weight loss, or at least she didn't comment on it. She had dark circles under her eyes and didn't seem to remember how to smile. Earl had lost his job at the motorcycle shop, which meant that instead of having the financial help she had counted on, Mom now had one more person to care for and one more mouth to feed.

Within a few hours of being home, the stiffness had returned to my body and my headache was back.

But it went away when I was at school. And at school, everyone noticed my weight loss, especially my gym teacher.

As I did three months before, I waited in a single file line with the other girls while Mrs. Shipley motioned for us to step onto the scale. When it was my turn, she did a double take.

"You weigh eighty-eight pounds! You look great!"

I smiled as her voice echoed through the gym. This time, I wanted the other girls to hear.

10

. . .

Connie and I were in the living room folding laundry when Earl rounded the corner. It took only one look at the cruel smile inching its way across his face to know he was looking for a fight.

"That dog of yours is a complete waste," he started, locking his icy-blue eyes on Connie. "All it ever does is eat, crap, and dig up the yard."

Earl was always picking fights and sometimes we just ignored him. But Abbey was off-limits—we all knew that.

Connie shot daggers at Earl.

"Speak for yourself," she sneered, hatred caking her voice.

Connie had never been the affectionate type and couldn't stand it when people tried to hug her, but with Abbey, it was different. The dog was constantly licking her, snuggling up against her, or jumping up on her in excitement, and she couldn't get enough of it.

"You know what I'm going to do?" Earl bellowed, his voice rising to a high-pitched whine. "I'll tell you what I'm going to do. I'm going to get rid of it!"

Connie didn't miss a beat.

"If Abbey goes, I go!" she hissed.

Within seconds she was on her feet, heading for the door. Earl grabbed her by her shoulders, spun her around, and threw her down into our cloth-covered rocking chair. Connie's body hit the chair with such force it nearly flipped over.

Earl hovered over her, ready to strike. But when the chair rocked back up, Connie had her feet in front of her and kicked him in the face, sending his glasses flying.

While he staggered around fumbling for his glasses, Connie jumped out of the chair and shot past him.

"Look what your daughter did now!" Earl screamed to Mom, who came running down the hallway just in time to see Connie slam the front door behind her.

Mom swung the door open and called after her. "Don't forget you have to be at the bishop's office at seven."

Her voice was calm and normal, like she hadn't overheard the eruption that had taken place.

Two hours later, our family crowded into Bishop Jones's office for what Mom told us would be a "family talk."

Bishop Jones stood at least six foot four and towered over the rest of us. He had broad shoulders and a big head with black hair and stern eyes. Even when he was sitting down, he took up a lot of space—especially in his cramped office, which barely fit his desk, a bookcase, a filing cabinet, and a couple of chairs.

It was late October and the outside air was so cold we all wore coats. But as soon as we jammed our seven bodies into the tiny, windowless space, it got hot and stuffy, accentuating Earl's stench. Whatever we were going to talk about, I wanted to get it started and over with so we could get out of that room.

I shot an annoyed look at the bishop, who was making small talk with Mom. Every time Mom had a problem, she ran to him for advice. It had driven Dad crazy when they were married. Bishop Jones knew every detail of Dad and Mom's relationship, all from Mom's point of view. He was the one who had overseen Dad's excommunication from the church and had advised Mom to get a divorce.

Dad couldn't stand Bishop Jones, and because of that I didn't like him either. Plus he was a hypocrite as far as Connie and I were concerned. We spotted him drinking what looked like coffee while walking by JB's Big Boy once. Coffee was forbidden because it violated the "Word of Wisdom" doctrine written (through revelation) by Joseph Smith, the first prophet and founder of the Mormon Church.

Bishop Jones stopped talking with Mom and stared at my siblings and me from across his desk, as if he could intimidate us into submission.

When he finally spoke, his tone was scolding and cold.

"Do you know how lucky you kids are that your mother has found someone who loves her and cares about her?" he asked, pausing for a moment to let his words penetrate. "Your mom and Earl are working hard to create a loving, stable life for you kids and you need to start supporting them in their efforts."

He glared at us, oozing self-righteousness. I wanted to scratch his eyes out.

"Yeah, aren't we all so lucky to be treated like dirt in our own house?" I wanted to scream. "Isn't it great that Mom now has a leech to support while he bosses her around and acts like she's his slave?"

I bit my lip and forced my body to stay still and my face to remain emotionless. I wasn't going to let this jerk get the best of me.

Bishop Jones spent the next ten minutes droning on about our responsibilities in the new family Mom and Earl were trying to create. After a while, I stopped listening. I found a spot on his oversized forehead and stared at it so Mom would think I was paying attention. When he finished preaching to us, he told all of us kids to wait in the foyer outside his office while he had a private conversation with Mom and Earl.

"No wonder Dad hates him so much," I fumed to Connie as soon as we were outside his office walls.

When the two of them came out five minutes later, Earl was gloating.

"Ingrid and Connie, Bishop Jones wants to talk to the two of you alone," Mom said in the serious, reverent tone she reserved for church. "We'll see you at home."

I was too pissed off to answer.

I looked over at Connie, who rolled her eyes in annoyance. I wondered if she was second-guessing herself for listening to Mom and coming to this family meeting.

Connie was sixteen now and had recently started her junior year of high school. Between basketball, track, and her job at the park, she was hardly ever home and usually managed to avoid the daily nightmare the rest of us experienced.

"I don't have time for this crap," she muttered as we headed back into Bishop Jones's office.

Bishop Jones was seated on his throne behind his desk and motioned for Connie and me to sit on the two metal folding chairs he had positioned in the five feet of space between the front of his desk and the wall.

He wasted no time making his point.

"I hear from your mom that you two girls are causing problems at home. What I don't understand is why."

He said this as a statement, not a question. It was clear from the way he was glaring down at us that we were to keep our mouths shut and listen.

His voice took on a hissing sound. "I want to tell you girls something right now. Your dad is no good. He was kicked out of the church for a reason. He was unfaithful to your mother and he hasn't been there for any of you in years."

I felt the blood rushing to my face. I looked at Connie for a cue. She had the bishop locked in a cold stare. Her brown eyes looked darker than I'd ever seen them.

He continued his verbal lashing. "You girls are lucky your mom found Earl, and you need to start loving and respecting him. After everything your dad's done, you don't even have a right to love him."

Connie wasn't all that close to Dad. But this put her over the edge. "Let me make sure I heard you right," she seethed, jumping out of her seat and leaning in toward the bishop. "Did you just tell us we don't have a right to love our dad?"

Before he could respond, Connie was grabbing the doorknob. I was right behind her. We walked out of his office door and then started running to the nearest church exit. Once outside, we sprinted for another block before stopping to catch our breath.

"What a jerk!" I huffed. "I hate him."

"I don't know who he thinks he is," Connie agreed, breathing hard. "I can't believe Mom set us up for that."

I was so grateful to Connie for standing up to Bishop Jones that I wanted to hug her. I wanted to thank her and tell her that I was glad she was my sister. I even considered telling her I loved her. But I knew she wouldn't go for any of that and I didn't want to ruin the moment.

"Yeah, I can't either," I said quietly.

We were both too worked up to go home so we began weaving up and down blocks in our neighborhood. The sky was dark and the air was freezing, but I felt safe and even warm next to Connie. She had proven that she would protect us even if Mom wouldn't.

We walked in silence for more than an hour. I didn't want to go anywhere near our house, and if Connie had wanted to, I would have stayed out all night. I was half hoping she would suggest we run away. But as the adrenaline rush wore off, the freezing air closed in on us.

"We should probably head back," she said finally. "But don't worry. If Mom asks any questions about the bishop meeting, I'll do the talking."

"Okay," I said, feeling a knot forming in my stomach.

When we got home, we were both relieved to see that all the

house lights were off—even the porch light. We walked in and made a beeline to our rooms.

Heidi didn't fight back against Earl like Connie and I did. She mainly stayed quiet and kept to herself. But ever since his arrival, the asthma she had been diagnosed with a couple of years before had gotten worse. After a while, her medication stopped working, and the week before Christmas, her breathing got so bad that she was admitted to the hospital.

On Christmas morning, we took our presents to her hospital room and opened them there, while she lay in bed, hooked up to tubes and a breathing machine.

She was so sick we had to open her presents for her.

Once back at home, Mom summoned all of us kids into the living room for a talk. Earl stayed hidden in the bedroom.

She looked tired and resigned.

"The doctor told me that Heidi's asthma is being caused by emotional problems and says we need to get some help. So I've made an appointment for family counseling."

I wanted to shake her until she came to her senses. We didn't need some counselor to tell us how to fix our family problems. We all knew what the problem was.

I considered voicing my thoughts but Mom looked so sad and defeated that I kept my mouth shut. Connie must have been thinking the same thing because she didn't speak up either.

A few days after Heidi was released from her two-week stay at the hospital—which Connie and I had secretly dubbed "her vacation" because of the break she got from home—we all headed for the Family Counseling Center, a free service sponsored by the Mormon Church.

We entered a plain, tan-brick building and walked into a large rectangular room with gray office carpet and glaring white walls. The room was empty except for eight metal chairs that had been arranged in a circle.

"Welcome," the counselor said, shaking Earl's hand and giving Mom a friendly pat on the back. "Why don't you all take a seat and we'll get started."

The counselor looked to be in his mid-forties and could have passed for any of the elders at church. He had a plain, clean-shaven face with thinning blond-brown hair that he wore combed over to one side of his head. He was medium height and had a slim frame that was dressed in a white, short-sleeve button-down shirt with a tie, and navy blue suit pants held up by a thin, black belt.

I followed Connie's lead and took a seat at the farthest end of the circle. Mom and Earl sat down in the chairs on either side of the counselor, who had positioned himself directly across from Connie and me. Heidi sat next to me, and Jacob and Daniel filled in the remaining seats.

For several minutes, no one spoke. Then the counselor started in.

"What's wrong with you kids?" he asked, looking directly at Connie and me. "Don't you know your mother and Earl are trying hard to make a nice family for all of you? Why can't you children show Earl a little love and respect? Don't you think your mother deserves that after all she has been through?"

resew it in an intricate zigzag pattern that works better with the muscles in your face.

"You'll still have a little scarring but it won't be nearly as noticeable. And when you smile, people won't even know it's there."

The doctor gave me a warm smile and patted my leg. His words were magic but I didn't want to get up my hopes. I looked at Mom, praying in my head that she would say yes.

"Would she have to go to the hospital?" Mom asked.

"Not at all," the doctor replied. "We can do this in our office in a couple of hours, and once it heals, she'll be as good as new."

"Okay. I want to schedule it," Mom said in a determined voice.

I was floating when we walked out of the office. I didn't know how Mom was going to afford it, but I couldn't ask because I didn't want to risk changing her mind.

"Thank you so much, Mom," I said, hugging her for the first time since she'd married Earl. "This means so much to me."

Mom hugged me back and I felt her tears on my neck. "I'm glad I can do this for you," she said.

A week later, Mom took me for the procedure. When the stitches were removed, the thick scar was gone, replaced with a thin, jagged line. The doctor was right. When I smiled, the scar wasn't even noticeable.

I felt pretty again and could actually stand to look at myself in the mirror. I also felt reconnected to Mom. But her kindness couldn't begin to counter Earl, and I was already making plans for my summer with Dad. I didn't ask Mom for permission to go with him anymore. It was now a given that as soon as school got out, I would be with him.

Dad's tool business had fizzled during the school year and he was back on the road selling tools with his revolving sales crew. He had recently moved out of his Salt Lake City office and had given up the mobile home he was renting; but he was still dating Rhonda and came to Utah every few weeks to visit her and see my siblings and me.

In May, Dad stopped by to tell us he and Rhonda had gotten married.

"Can you believe it? Now I've got three more daughters," he said with a laugh. "Yeah, I don't know how I'm going to survive with all the estrogen floating around me. But I'm pretty sure Natalie's fine with it. She just talked me into buying her a horse."

Dad's words stung. The only present he had ever bought me was the jade bracelet he gave me when he and Mom were getting divorced. How could he buy her a horse?

I tried to swallow my jealousy and convince myself that it was important for Dad to build a good relationship with Natalie. But Connie couldn't hide her devastation.

"Well, can I have a horse too?" she blurted. She looked like the air had been knocked out of her, and for the first time I could remember, I actually thought she was going to cry. Connie had fantasized about a horse ever since the one time Dad took her riding when she was five.

If Dad noticed Connie's heartache, he didn't show it.

"You got the car," he replied with a shrug, referring to the navy blue, two-door Honda Civic hatchback he had given her a few months before. "I'd say that's the better end of the deal."

Dad rarely gave Mom money for child support. He justified it by arguing that he didn't want to support Earl. Instead, he decided that when each of us kids turned sixteen, he would give us a car. The car, Dad said, would belong just to us and would help set us free from the hell at home.

Connie loved her car. The only problem was that Mom needed a reliable car for work. Mom traveled as much as fifty miles a day visiting patients in their homes around the valley. Her junked up Impala was constantly breaking down and got horrible gas mileage. When she realized that Connie's Honda got thirty miles to the gallon, she asked if she could use it.

Connie didn't want to give up her prize possession. But she knew Mom needed it so she reluctantly agreed—meaning that her car was actually only hers on the weekend.

Connie didn't explain the car situation to Dad. And she never mentioned the horse again. She just tucked away the hurt deep inside herself, like she always did, and continued on with her life.

Nine years later, she was rushed to the hospital with a perforated ulcer and had to undergo emergency surgery to patch the hole in her stomach. The doctor who operated on her said he had never seen an ulcer that had eaten itself all the way through the stomach lining in someone so young. He warned Connie that if she didn't stop internalizing her pain and stress, she would die.

11

. . .

Dad picked me up the morning after school let out and said we were headed to Rhonda's house, where we would stay for a day or two before leaving for Dallas, Texas.

Texas was where he had decided to set up his new business headquarters.

"Let me tell you something, Ingrid," Dad said as we drove the ninety miles from Logan to Salt Lake City. "That's where the money is and that's where I'm gonna get rich."

Dad explained that a huge oil boom was going on in the Midwest and said boomtowns were popping up everywhere. The best part of that, he said, was that migrant workers were coming up from Mexico to work the oil rigs and were easy prospects.

"I've got my whole sales crew out there working the boomtowns and you wouldn't believe how the money is flying. It's like the gold rush they had in California in the 1800s. It's crazy."

Dad reached over and patted my leg. He was clearly on a high and his mood was infectious.

"So do you want to hear how your daddy is capitalizing on it all? Here's what I do, Ingrid. I go to the Dallas–Fort Worth area—that's where all these wholesale tool warehouses are located—and I stock up on a bunch of tools and give them to my guys on consignment. Then they go work these boomtowns and oil rigs throughout Kansas and Oklahoma and a few days later, they return with a pile of cash and I restock them. And I always figure in a ten to fifteen percent margin for myself for supplying them with the tools."

"That's great, Dad," I said, feeling his excitement. "Sounds like a perfect setup."

"Let me tell you something, Ingrid, it really is the perfect setup. See, this way I don't have to carry an inventory like I did when I was working here in Utah. That was my problem. Plus I had to pay for shipping costs. Now I've cut out all of that expense. I just give the guys tools on consignment, wait until they are running low, and then use the money from the sales to buy more tools.

"Can you imagine how fast that money can add up?" he continued. "I tell you what, Ingrid, I know I've said it before, but your daddy is going to be a millionaire someday. And at the rate we're going, it's going to happen sooner than you think."

I was so happy to be free of Earl and the suffocating rules in our house that just being in the truck with Dad was enough to make me want to start shouting hallelujahs out the window. But Dad's story about all the money flying in Texas had my heart pounding.

"I always knew you could do it," I said, sliding over on the vinyl bench seat so I could give him a squeeze. "Texas sounds incredible. I can't wait to get there."

We made it to Salt Lake City and headed for Rhonda's house, a beige split-level located in a run-down neighborhood on the south side of the city. I was nervous about camping out at a stranger's house and I worried about how Dad's new marriage would interfere with our time together. I was also nervous about how I would get along with Rhonda's daughters. But within a few hours, I relaxed. Rhonda was quiet, but nice to me and didn't seem at all possessive of Dad. And her daughters weren't even around. When I asked Dad about it, he said Natalie was staying at a friend's house but would fly out to Texas with Rhonda in a couple of weeks, after he and I got established.

"Andrea and Dana both live with their boyfriends so they won't be coming," he added. "I'll tell you something, Ingrid. I'm sure glad you don't have boyfriends yet. It's their life, but in my book, they are way too young to be shacking up with guys."

Within a couple of days, Dad and I were on our way. I hadn't left the state since our move to Mississippi in the third grade and couldn't wait to hit the road.

Before pulling out of the driveway, Dad handed me a road atlas and said I could be the navigator.

"We're a team, you know," he said as we turned onto the interstate. "I might be the one behind the wheel, but you're the one who's going to figure out how to get us there."

I knew Dad had driven the route plenty of times, but I was proud to have a job to do and took it seriously. I took out a pencil and carefully plotted our route down through New Mexico and the Texas panhandle.

"So tell me about Dallas," I prodded as we drove, searching through the music stations on the truck radio.

"Oh, it's something else, Ingrid. There are so many buildings and skyscrapers it makes Salt Lake City look like nothing. See, it's not just one big city, there's two of them. Dallas is the big city but Fort Worth is only thirty miles away and it's a pretty good-sized city on its own. The airport that sits between the two of them is so big it's like a little city in itself."

Dad and I drove until it was late and spent the night at a roadside motel in Amarillo, Texas.

The next afternoon, we made it to the Dallas area.

Though Dad had described it, I couldn't hide the rush I felt as I took in the city buzz around me. Glass skyscrapers were everywhere and the highways that looped through the city were so packed with cars it almost made me dizzy.

"So what do you think, Ingrid? Think you can make this your home for a while?"

"YES!" I almost shouted. "Definitely."

"Well, that's good. Because I'm going to need your help picking us out a place to live."

Dad looped around the city so I could get an up-close look. But instead of staying in the downtown area, he headed to Arlington, a connector town located between Dallas and Fort Worth. As soon as we arrived, he found a Motel 6 for us to check into and purchased a local paper from the newspaper vending machine.

Then we headed to our room.

"What do you say we start planning our future," Dad said, handing me the paper and a pen he pulled out from his shirt pocket.

"Why don't you look through the rental section and circle all the apartments that look good to you. Just make sure that it has at least two bedrooms and doesn't cost more than four hundred dollars a month. That's our maximum budget."

I couldn't believe Dad trusted me to help find a place to live. I looked up and saw him smiling at me.

"Like I told you, we're a team," he said. "Your opinion is every bit as important as mine. And I know you'll make sure we have something that Rhonda and Natalie are going to like. You've got a better understanding of female tastes."

"That's for sure." I replied with a laugh.

I plopped down on one of the double beds, spread open the newspaper to the classifieds, and began combing through the "For Rent" ads, looking for apartments that had at least two bedrooms and a swimming pool. One thing I had already discovered about Dallas—it was scorching hot. And the air had so much humidity in it that just walking from Dad's pickup to the room had made me sweat.

I knew a swimming pool was going to feel nice to all of us. Plus I was already thinking about all the fun Natalie and I were going to have once she arrived.

I spent the next hour scouring the ads and circling the ones that sounded good while Dad headed to a nearby pay phone to make some calls to his sales crew. When he returned to the room, I had ten possibilities.

"Look at that," Dad said, glancing through my selections. "I knew I was in good hands with you."

Dad checked out the addresses on the apartment complexes I had found and eliminated six of them because the locations weren't right. That left us four possibilities.

"Well, what are we waiting for?" he said, jumping up from the bed. "Let's go check them out."

On the way to the truck, he stopped by the lobby soda machine and bought a couple of Sugar Free Dr Peppers. It was Dad's favorite and was quickly becoming my favorite too.

"This will give us the extra kick we need," he said, tossing one my way. We stopped by a gas station for a street map and began making our way to the apartments. Even from the outside, we could tell we didn't like the first apartment complex. The lawn was brown and overgrown, and Dad said that was the first sign of problems. But as soon as we reached the second one and pulled into the complex parking lot, we both knew we had found our home.

"Well, this is nice," Dad said, taking in the acres of green, landscaped lawns. "I'd say it's beautiful, wouldn't you? Why don't we take a walk around?"

The apartment complex looked new, with several buildings sprawled across the green grass. Automatic sprinklers were going off everywhere and I thought it must cost them a fortune to keep the grass so green. Dad loved the palm trees that dotted the grounds, making it look like a tropical island. But what caught my attention was the enormous outdoor swimming pool with a diving board that sat in the center courtyard. It was surrounded by lounge chairs, and a few residents were lying out on them with a book or a drink. Next to the pool was a tennis court. It was what I imagined a luxury hotel would look like.

"This place is so perfect!" I shouted, running over to the pool to take a closer look. "I hope they have a two-bedroom left. I hope, I hope, I hope. And I hope they'll rent it to us."

I was on such a high I was almost dizzy.

"Oh, don't worry about that, Ingrid," Dad said, chuckling. "If they've got an apartment available, it's ours. Nobody can say no to me. Don't you know that about your daddy by now?"

We headed back to the main parking lot and found a set of glass doors with the word "Office" stenciled on them. The woman smiled warmly at us when we walked in and asked us if we would like a tour of the two bedroom apartment she had available. An hour later, Dad and I walked out with the keys and a rental agreement.

We relaxed that night and checked out of our motel the following morning. Now that we had our housing nailed down, Dad said it was time to search for office space. Dad hadn't said so the day before, but one of the things he had liked about our new apartment was that it was close to several strip malls and he had seen a couple of "For Lease" signs while we were driving by them.

That's where we headed, and by noon Dad had secured office space at a small strip mall storefront located two blocks from a movie theater. It was also less than a mile from our new apartment.

"You know what I think, Ingrid?" Dad said as we climbed back into the truck. "I think you're good luck. That's what I think."

I laughed. It was hard to believe that only a few days before, I was sitting at the dinner table waiting for Earl to allow me to speak. The change was so night and day it was like I had entered another planet.

Dad and I headed to a nearby McDonald's for a lunch break. Afterward we went to Kmart to load up on house and office supplies. When we entered the store, Dad motioned for me to grab a shopping cart. He grabbed one as well.

"We're probably going to need another basket before it's all through, but why don't you get started on bedding and dishes while I hunt down office supplies."

I loved shopping with Dad. He gave me free reign over the household department and agreed with anything I chose. Whenever I asked him what he thought of something, he put it back on me.

"If you like it, that's all that matters," he said. "You're the boss."

By the end of our shopping trip, I had picked out sheets, blankets, towels, shower curtains, pillows, dishes, and a variety of kitchen cleaning supplies. Along with office supplies, Dad picked out a small TV set so we had some entertainment.

The next day, while I was busy getting the apartment set up, Dad purchased a queen-size mattress and metal bed frame for him and Rhonda. He also picked up a couple of foam mats for Natalie and me, and said we could use those for a while until he had the money to buy real beds for us.

Rhonda and Natalie arrived at the end of the week. Natalie was five foot seven—a good five inches taller than me—and had a perfect, thin body and long, dark hair. I knew from what Dad told me that she had a lot more experience in everything than I did. She had tasted alcohol and had already been on dates—something I wasn't allowed to do until I turned sixteen.

I wasn't sure how we would get along, but we hit it off immediately. "Why don't we pretend we're sisters?" Natalie suggested that evening as we headed to the swimming pool. "I mean, we practically are."

Natalie and I spent the next two weeks living like we were at some tropical vacation resort. Most mornings, we got up around 9 A.M., ate breakfast, and then headed to the swimming pool for a few hours while Dad and Rhonda were at the office. In the afternoon, the two of us lounged around the apartment watching TV. In the evening, we helped Rhonda make dinner and then headed back to the pool or relaxed in front of the television set with Dad and Rhonda.

I was just getting used to my new leisure lifestyle when Rhonda received a phone call notifying her that Andrea had been rushed to the hospital with a tubal pregnancy. The next morning, we drove her and Natalie to the airport so they could catch a flight back to Utah.

"Well, Ingrid, I sure wasn't counting on that expense, I'll tell you that," Dad muttered as we headed from the airport to the office.

I hadn't spent much time with Dad during the two weeks that Natalie and Rhonda were in town and hadn't realized how bad our money situation had become. As soon as we arrived at the office, Dad began making calls to the three guys on his sales crew. I didn't have to overhear much to get the picture.

"Now you listen to me," Dad yelled into the phone. "I have

got to get some money in here. Do you realize what kind of expenses I've got to cover? I've fronted you all of these tools and need the sales so I can keep things afloat. If you're not going to sell anything, give my merchandise back to me and I'll find someone who will!"

Dad spent the afternoon pacing through his office. That evening, he announced that we were heading out on the road to sell.

"I guess they can't sell without me showing them how it's done," Dad fumed. "So I better head out there and set an example."

As much as I had been enjoying my time at the apartment, I was always up for an adventure, and hitting the road sounded like fun. When I asked Dad what we were going to do about the apartment and office, he said we'd just keep them both and use them as our base when we came back to Texas to restock on merchandise.

"What about Rhonda and Natalie?" I asked. "Are they coming back out after Andrea's feeling better?"

Dad shook his head.

"I think they'll just stay put in Utah for a while. Rhonda's more of a homebody anyway—and if I'm going to be back on the road selling tools, she'd rather be in her own house and near her daughters."

The next morning, we packed up our bags and drove to a wholesale warehouse in Fort Worth. Dad had equipped the back of his truck with a small camper where he stored the wrench sets, metric socket sets, screwdrivers, hammers, and kitchen knives he purchased. By noon, we were on our way to Oklahoma.

I had always envied Dad's freewheeling sales life and now that I finally had a chance to join him, I wanted to make myself valuable. I'd been thinking about my role since the night before and decided I could be most useful in a support capacity.

"I think I should be your sales organizer," I announced as soon as we turned the truck onto the interstate. "I mean, you're going to need someone to keep track of sales and map out where we're going."

"You know what, Ingrid, I think you are exactly right," Dad said, patting my leg like he always did. "I guess the first thing we need to do is figure out how much we need to make."

He pulled over to a McDonald's so we could get something to eat and figure out some things. While we chewed on our Big Macs, Dad began working out the numbers.

"I figure if I'm doing the selling, we can average a thirty percent margin. Assuming I can still count on a little commission from my sales crew, I'd say we need to make a profit of one hundred and fifty dollars a day to cover our expenses and my obligations. So if that's the case, how much do we need to gross each day?"

I quickly worked the math problem in my head. "Five hundred dollars."

Dad busted out laughing.

"You're going to be a good sales organizer, Ingrid. I know that much already. I'm wondering how I ever managed without you.

"So that you have all the facts on the table, you should know that I only average about twenty-five dollars per sale, so we're looking at twenty sales a day." Dad let out a whistle. "That's a lot of sales. What do you think, Ingrid? Think we can do that?"

I could tell this talk was just what Dad needed to get motivated and I was determined to get us back on track.

"Of course we can do it," I replied in the most motivational voice I could muster. "You're the best, right? But we're going to need to keep track of our sales, so I'm going to need a notebook." Dad laughed again.

"Okay, boss. Let's do it."

After finishing lunch, we drove a few blocks until we found a 7-Eleven. Dad grabbed our Sugar Free Dr Peppers while I picked out an orange spiral-bound notebook and a packet of Bic pens. Once back in the truck, I wrote the words "Tool Sales" in large bubble letters across the front of the notebook.

As Dad drove, I started formulating our plan of attack. I knew from our conversations that the first one hundred dollars in sales was always the hardest to secure, so I decided we should make it a rule that we couldn't stop for breakfast until we had reached that sales benchmark.

"This way, we're already a fifth of the way there," I explained to Dad. "Plus, if we start early, we can knock out some sales before it gets so hot."

Dad shook his head.

"You want to know something? I think you're made for this lifestyle. And you're absolutely right about getting started early. I always say the early bird catches the worm."

Since we had gotten such a late start, we decided to take it easy for the rest of the day and checked into a twenty-three-dollar-a-night roadside motel I had spotted. The next morning, we started a routine that would become our daily ritual.

Dad, who never slept past 5 A.M., woke me up as soon as he was awake. To get the blood flowing, we spent fifteen minutes running laps around the motel and then finished our workout with a hundred jumping jacks and twenty sit-ups. Then I hopped into the shower so I could spend a few minutes blow-drying my hair and getting in a few curls with my curling iron while Dad had his turn in the shower.

It was my job to pack up our bags and return the motel room key to the front desk while Dad loaded up the truck with the tools we'd carried into the motel room the night before for safe-keeping. By 6 A.M., we were in the truck and on the road.

"What's our saying?" Dad yelled, letting his voice carry into the still early morning hour.

"The early bird catches the worm!" I shouted back.

To kick off the day right, Dad and I grabbed a Sugar Free Dr Pepper from the gas station where we filled up the tank and checked the oil.

Then we were on our way.

Within a week, I had our sales routine down pat. And our early morning start became the most important component. It didn't take long to learn that the midday heat made people cranky and that our prospects were in much better moods and were much more likely to buy when the air was crisp and the day was still fresh. This was important because the first sale of the day was always the toughest and Dad needed an early success to give him the lift and confidence to keep going.

Our first few sales stops always set the tone for the day. If Dad made a sale to the first or second guy he approached, I knew it was going to be a good day and that we stood a reasonable chance of wrapping up early and treating ourselves to an afternoon of lounging in our motel room, watching TV, or just relaxing while the cool air from the air conditioner washed over us. If Dad encountered three "nos" straight out of the gate, I mentally braced myself for the long hours ahead.

Our sales strategy consisted of driving the secondary roads throughout Oklahoma, Arkansas, Kansas, and Iowa, looking for prospects. We kept our eyes peeled for the lone gas station attendant or the do-it-yourself mechanic working on his car. But what we were most interested in were the oil-rig job sites where, at any given time, a group of two or three migrant workers could be found taking a smoke break or digging into the sandwiches they'd brought from home.

"These guys have so much money in their pockets they're just waiting for an opportunity to spend it," Dad would say as we pulled up to a job site. "Well, they're about to get their chance."

Whenever Dad or I spotted what looked like a good prospect, Dad parked the truck, hopped out, and initiated a conversation.

"Is it hot enough for ya today?" he would ask, or "I think it's quitting time, don't you?"

If the guy responded in a positive way, Dad would make small talk for a couple more minutes to warm him up and then casually mention that he was liquidating some tools and ask if the guy would like to take a look.

I always waited for the signal to bring out some merchandise. Sometimes Dad just looked over at the truck and gave me a quick nod. Other times, it boiled down to time.

"If I'm still gone after five minutes, bring me a wrench set," he would say as he left the truck.

When it was time, I grabbed the agreed upon tools out of the back of the truck, ran to Dad's side, and flashed my warmest smile. When our prospect saw that Dad had his daughter with him, it usually softened the guy up, and he was willing to spend twenty dollars, even if he didn't need a wrench set.

Our truck didn't have air-conditioning and by mid-morning, I was always covered in sweat. My legs stuck to the vinyl seat of the truck and I was constantly shifting positions to get comfortable. Dad caked on his Old Spice aftershave each morning to hide the sweat-induced body odor that kicked in after a few hours in the baking heat; by the end of our day, we were both sweaty and dirty from the hot dust that kicked up on us when we stepped out near the oil rigs to talk with our prospects. But despite the discomfort, I loved life on the road with Dad. It felt natural to me, and for the first time in my life, I felt like I belonged.

When we did reach that first one hundred dollar mark each morning, Dad and I celebrated with a trip through the drive-through window at the first McDonald's we came across for a quick Egg McMuffin and orange juice. Lunch usually consisted of a Hostess CupCake and Sugar Free Dr Pepper from a 7-Eleven or gas station.

"This is the life, isn't it?" Dad would say with a grin as we kicked back in the air-conditioned room for a few minutes with our ice-cold drinks and sugar treats.

Each time Dad made a sale, I carefully noted in my orange spiral-bound notebook what tools he had sold and for what price. Then I calculated our profit and recorded that number in a separate column. I also kept a running total of the sales so Dad would know how much more we needed to sell to reach our daily goal.

"So where are we at?" Dad would always ask a few hours into the day. "Have we hit our halfway point yet?"

Although my official job was smiling at prospects and keeping track of our sales and profits, I quickly realized my most important task was to keep Dad on target. If he got tired and needed rest, it was my job to make sure he napped for only twenty minutes. If he got discouraged, it was my job to cheer him up. And if it was getting late and Dad was still one hundred dollars short of our daily goal, it was my job to push him along, coaxing him into making one more stop so that we could reach our five hundred dollar goal.

My words of encouragement usually encompassed some sort of a deal.

"I'll tell you what, Dad. Let's just make three more stops and see what happens. I'll bet the next guy you talk to buys something. We only need to sell four more sets of wrenches to meet our goal."

This was all it ever took. A tired smile would creep across his face. I knew he was in when I saw his hands grip the steering wheel with renewed determination.

"Really, that's all we need to sell? Just four more wrench sets? Okay, you're the boss. Let's do it."

My emotions mirrored Dad's. When he scored an easy sale and doubled our usual profit margin, it put us both on a high. When he encountered a string of "no"s, I shared his disappointment. A rude comment to Dad could deflate me or send me into an angry rage. Most of the time it wasn't what our prospects said, but how they said it—and how they looked at Dad when they talked.

"Look, if I want to buy something, I'll just go to the store," a guy would say, eyeing both Dad and me with disdain. Other times, guys would tell Dad flat-out that they weren't interested in buying "hot" merchandise, implying that Dad was some sort of a criminal.

"Well, Ingrid, he was a first-rate bastard," Dad would fume, slamming the truck door closed and pushing down hard on the gas pedal. "There's just no reason to treat people like that."

At those times I would reach for Dad's hand and squeeze it to show my support. I fought back the hot humiliation that surged through me as I worked to comfort Dad and rebuild his spirits.

"They're just jealous, Dad. That's all. They're just pissed off about being tied to a nine-to-five job."

Though Dad had said we could keep the Texas apartment as our home base, I knew he was struggling to keep up the rent. The next time we were in Dallas to stock up on tools, Dad told me to pack up the dishes and bedding from the apartment so we could store it in the office.

"Why do we need an apartment when we've got the open road to call our home?" Dad said after returning the apartment keys to the office manager. "Apartments just confine us."

I couldn't help but feel bad because I had started fantasizing about living with Dad permanently, and I knew that without a regular place to live, that was out the window. But I also knew that money wasn't flying in the way Dad had said it was.

We nearly always reached our five hundred dollar daily goal when we were working, but it was becoming clear to me that one hundred and fifty dollars a day wasn't enough. If the truck broke down and Dad had to spend the day fixing it, or any other unexpected expenses came up, it immediately put us in the hole. Along with covering the office lease and gas and living expenses on the road, Dad was also supposed to send money to Rhonda, who had quit her job as a grocery clerk when she and Dad married. Then there was the mounting child support he owed Mom.

Every time Dad called home to talk with the other kids, Mom grabbed the receiver and berated him for not paying child support.

"The next time your mom mentions something about child support, tell her that she ought to be sending me child support during the summer to take care of you," he would rage after slamming down the phone.

I knew Dad was just blowing off steam but I hated feeling caught in the middle between him and Mom. I understood now that despite Dad's argument of not wanting to support Earl, the truth was that he rarely had the money to cover his child support obligation. But I also knew how desperately Mom needed the child support, and I started panicking about all the money I was costing Dad—which in turn made it harder for him to pay Mom.

Though we ate cheaply, I estimated that the cost for my food alone came to nearly fifteen dollars a day, and I knew that if it weren't for me, Dad would be spending more of his nights sleeping in the back of the truck instead of renting a room at Motel 6, which cost us between thirty and forty dollars a night. Dad had fired what he referred to as his "piece of shit" sales crew when we started selling ourselves in mid-June. But by early August, the money pressure was getting to be so great that Dad decided the only way out was to find guys to sell for him again.

"I just need to multiply what we're doing sales-wise and we'll have so much money coming in we won't know what to do with it," Dad said, explaining his plan to me. "Yup, Ingrid. That's the answer."

Dad decided to act immediately by placing a Help Wanted ad in the newspaper in Oklahoma City. We headed to a McDonald's so I could help him write a "Make $1,000 a Week, No Experience Necessary" ad. But before we could run it, Dad said we had to rent a motel room so he had a place to receive calls and conduct interviews. He decided to book a room at a Red Lion for three days.

"We've got to have a nice room to impress the sales guys who turn up for an interview," Dad explained when I questioned the wisdom of spending so much for lodging.

I understood Dad's reasoning, but I was worried. The room at the Red Lion was costing us more than twice as much as a room at the Motel 6, and I knew that each day we took off from selling meant going further into the hole financially.

After thinking about it for a few hours, I decided the only answer was for me to do some selling on my own.

"Here's what I'm thinking," I told Dad the evening we ran

the ad. "While you're in here finding guys for your sales crew, I'll set up a table at the stop light across the parking lot and make a few sales."

Dad looked relieved. "Now why didn't I think of that?" he said as we carried in our merchandise from the truck for the evening. "That's one of the best ideas I've heard all day."

The next morning, I put on my favorite shorts and tank top, and then spent an hour curling my hair and carefully applying layers of mascara and eye shadow. I knew I needed to look good if I wanted to get guys to stop at my table. I also hoped it would make me look older than fourteen.

Dad whistled when he saw me. "Well, I think you are going to stop them in their tracks."

I rolled my eyes. "Just doing what it takes," I said as I walked out the door.

I headed to the front desk and talked the desk clerk into letting me borrow a card table and folding chair from the motel conference room. Then I dragged them across the hotel parking lot to the corner of a busy intersection. Dad followed behind me with a box full of wrench sets, screwdrivers, and several sets of steak knives.

I arranged them on the table and then took a seat, ready for business. The four-way intersection was packed with cars, and men whistled and yelled as they drove by me. I always smiled sweetly and waved, hoping it would get them to stop. Mostly they just kept on driving. But every once in a while, a guy would pull his car over to the side of the road and walk up to my table.

"Well, hello, gorgeous," he would say, eyeing me up and down as he spoke. "What you got here?"

"I've got what you need," I always replied, offering my prospect a flirtatious smile.

"Everyone needs an extra tool set for their car or truck," I continued. "What happens if you break down on the side of the road? And these knives have a lifetime guarantee. You don't even need to sharpen them."

By this point in my sales pitch, my prospect usually had an odd grin on his face. It must have been funny to see a teenage girl who barely topped five foot one and weighed ninety pounds standing at a busy street corner hawking tools. Just the experience was probably well worth the twenty dollars he would spend on the knives or tools. But I was convinced that I had inherited Dad's knack for selling and was certain I had my prospect eating out of the palm of my hand.

I always saved my ace for the end.

"I can give you a great deal on anything you see here," I would tell the guy, gracefully sweeping my arm across the goods displayed on the table like I had watched the models do on *The Price Is Right*. "And it would really help me out. I'm here working with my dad, trying to earn money for college."

If I could get a guy to stop by my table, I was usually successful in making a sale. But when he followed up by asking me on a date, I quickly passed.

"My dad won't let me," I would respond when pressed.

"Why do you need your daddy's approval, honey? How old are you anyway?"

"Sixteen," I would lie. "But my dad is very protective."

I operated my business for the next three days. Every few hours, Dad would take a break from his interviews and cross the parking lot to see how I was doing. He would bring me a cold Sugar Free Dr Pepper and cover me for a few minutes here and there so I could take a restroom break or grab something to eat. By the end of the three-day period, I had sold three hundred and ninety dollars' worth of merchandise. It was well short of our daily five hundred dollar goal, but it felt good to know that I had helped offset our expenses.

The best part was seeing the proud smile on Dad's face.

"Well, Ingrid, I think you're a natural," he said as we packed up the unsold merchandise and broke down the table the last day there. "We make a great team, don't we?"

12

· · ·

It was Monday night, the once a week time-slot designated by the Mormon Church as family night. Most families I knew used the night to go bowling together or would head to Baskin-Robbins for some ice cream. Our time was always spent in the living room, listening to some church lesson that Earl or Mom had prepared from the Family Home Evening lesson book.

I had only been back from my summer with Dad for a month, but it felt like I had been trapped in this suffocating prison forever.

After getting laid off from his motorcycle mechanic job, Earl had set up shop in our garage and did odd car repairs for people he hit up at church. As a result, he was always hanging around the house, making it impossible to escape him.

I now made a habit of hanging out after school each day and riding the activity bus home so I could avoid being around Earl when Mom wasn't home. Most nights I made it through dinner, knocked out the dinner dishes, and then spent the rest of the evening locked in the safety of my attic room. But on Monday nights, we were all trapped in the living room for at least two hours with Earl and there was no escape.

On this particular night, the evening's topic was obeying and respecting your parents, and Earl had taken over. He lorded over us from the green couch, quoting from the large lesson book spread open across his stubby thighs.

"'Thou shall obey thy father and mother,'" he read, glancing around at all of us for effect.

I had become an expert at zoning out. I usually found a speck on the wall just above Earl's head and focused all my attention there. It was amazing how many different shapes a speck could take on if you stared at it long enough.

After a few minutes Earl's drone stopped and I heard Mom's voice. "Ingrid, are you listening to me? I said we are going to start father-daughter talks!"

Her words were like needles pricking my skin and definitely got my attention. I don't know what had gotten into Mom during the three months I'd been away, but she seemed to have rededicated herself to her role as obedient Mormon wife and did everything Earl ordered her to do. She was starting to sound like Earl's mouthpiece.

"Earl has decided to implement one-on-one talks with all of you kids," she continued sternly. "I think it's a great idea. We need to start changing things around here."

I looked at her in disgust, but the alarm was sounding in my head. I didn't know what the two of them were up to, but I knew it wasn't good.

Earl stayed seated by her side on the green couch, not saying a word, just nodding his head in agreement. Every time he moved his head downward in a nodding motion, I could see flecks of dandruff caught in his greasy, matted black hair.

"We're going to do these on a weekly basis," Mom continued. "Ingrid, we've decided to start with you."

Of course they would start with me. I glanced over at Connie and Heidi, who didn't even try to hide their relief. I wanted to punch them both to wipe the smirks off their faces. My brothers snuggled next to Mom, free of the nightmare that awaited my sisters and me.

"Come on, Ingrid. Let's go."

I shot a final dirty look at Connie and Heidi before leaving the room, determined not to let them see the panic that was shooting through me.

I tried to get back into my zone-out state as I followed Mom and Earl into their bedroom, but I could feel the blood rushing to my face, and my heart was pounding too hard to relax. Just the thought of being in such close proximity to Earl made me want to puke. Mom's bedroom was tiny, and between the double bed and the dresser, there was only about two feet of moving room.

I took a seat on Mom's bed and glared at her and Earl. They both leaned up against the dresser in front of me.

"First of all, I would like you to address me as 'Father,'" Earl started out, locking his icy-blue eyes on me. "'Father' is a respectable name and I deserve it."

It was the same demand he had been making since he and Mom married a year and a half ago. It was clearly just a power play, since he had to have known by now I'd rather be chopped up into tiny pieces than utter that word.

"You are *not* my DAD!" I snarled. "You're Mom's husband. That's all!"

Earl turned to Mom. "Tell her to stop talking to me that way. Tell her. NOW!"

Mom grabbed my arm. I tried to shake her off but she was digging in hard with her fingers and wasn't about to let go.

"Ingrid! Stop it right now!"

"Just get away from me! Both of you!"

I thrashed around, trying to break free from her grasp. Then Earl grabbed me, pushed me backward, and helped Mom pin me to their bed.

"Ingrid, listen to me," Mom said, her voice suddenly filled with concern. "I think you have Satan inside of you. Earl's going to give you a blessing."

They still held me down on the bed, discussing where the sacred ointment was hidden so Earl could use his priesthood powers to bless the evil spirits out of me. Their voices became a muffled jumble around me. My head was pounding and I could hear a single word repeating itself in my mind: *Escape. Escape. Escape.*

Earl relaxed his hold. It was all I needed. I kicked him in the stomach, wrestled free from Mom, and ran from the room. I blocked out their yells as I reached for the front door, opened it, and slammed it behind me. I started sprinting down the block. I didn't know where I was going. I just knew I had to get away.

I ran a few blocks into the dark night and then stopped to catch my breath. It was early October and already the temperature hovered near freezing. I was wearing only a long-sleeved T-shirt and jeans.

I needed a plan. I didn't have a place to go and I was scared to venture too far from the house because the night was so dark I was having a hard time seeing anything.

The top half of our block was a large, overgrown weed patch nearly the length of a football field. I decided to head there and make it my hiding place until I could figure out what to do next. I retraced my steps back to my block and waded through the weeds into the center of the field. I used my hands to flatten some of the weeds, then plopped down and hugged my knees into my chest to keep warm. The weeds loomed about four feet high, and I figured I was safe for a while. I rocked back and forth, trying to comfort myself.

Once I had calmed down enough to think, I played out the situation in my mind—trying to come up with an answer. But no matter how many times I went over it, my dilemma never changed. Life at home was hell and I wanted and needed to be with Dad. But Dad lived on the road and I couldn't be with him unless I wanted to drop out of ninth grade. Dad and I had actually discussed the idea a few times during the summer, though we both knew it wasn't really an option. But this brought me right back to life with Mom and Earl, and I didn't know how much longer I could stand it.

I wondered if Mom was sorry about what had just happened and if she was worried about me. I half expected to hear her voice calling out to me and sat waiting for it to happen. I thought about how I would react. I wouldn't answer her calls at first; I would let her worry for a while and think about what she had just done. When I was convinced she was sorry, I would call out to her. She would make her way into the field, we would hug for a while, and she would tell me how scared she was that I was gone and how sorry she was for getting so weird on me.

I waited for nearly two hours, hoping to hear her voice. But the only sounds I heard were my teeth chattering and the crickets chirping. I was freezing and alone. I couldn't stand the thought of going back home, but it was too cold to stay outside any longer and I had nowhere else to go.

I stood up and slowly made my way back to the house. The porch light was on but otherwise the house was dark. I turned the knob on the front door and was relieved to find it unlocked. Straining to be as quiet as possible, I stepped inside.

The house was silent. Everyone seemed to be sleeping. It was as if nothing had happened earlier and no one cared that I was gone.

I tiptoed to the attic entrance, scaled the plywood steps to my room, and quickly shut my door. Then I attached the hook lock, pushed my nightstand up against the door, and crawled into bed in my jeans and T-shirt. I wanted to be ready to run if need be.

Though finally warm under the covers, I couldn't stop my body from trembling. I stared at the ceiling for what felt like hours before I drifted off to sleep.

Before parting ways for the school year, Dad had given me a cloth calendar with his face silkscreened onto it so I had a ready reminder of him and could quickly count down the nine months until our reunion.

I had hung the calendar in my locker at school so I could see his smiling face in between classes. I missed him so much my gut ached and I worried about him constantly. Dad was a magnet for trouble. Once he had picked up a hitchhiker and barely escaped after being robbed at knifepoint. Another time he got caught in a flood in Iowa and nearly drowned. I didn't think I could bear it if something happened to him. Beyond losing him, I was petrified of being left without an escape route.

In late October, about three weeks after the Family Home Evening incident, Mom woke up all of us kids earlier than usual and summoned us into the living room for a talk.

She looked shaken.

"Your dad was taken hostage last night by a man who escaped from prison, but I just talked with him and he's fine." Mom's voice sounded concerned and her mouth was turned down into a frown. "He's at the police station right now answering some questions and then he's going to get some sleep, but he will call later tonight."

Hearing the words "Dad" and "hostage" in the same sentence was almost more than I could handle. My heart was pounding so hard against my chest, I thought it might break through my ribs. I couldn't believe what I was hearing. I had just talked with Dad around 5:30 the evening before and everything had been fine. Somehow, between the time I hung up the phone and now, he had been taken hostage by a convicted criminal and could have been killed.

"So what happened?" I nearly screamed at Mom. "What's going on?"

"I don't know," Mom admitted. "Your dad didn't have much time to talk. Maybe there's something about it on the news."

As if on cue, Earl walked into the living room and announced that it was time to read scriptures. For once, Mom had other things on her mind.

"The children want to find out what happened to their dad, and I think that's more important right now," she said firmly, hardly even looking at Earl. "We can skip scriptures this morning."

For whatever reason, Earl didn't argue. He just glared at all of us and stomped out of the room. Mom turned on the TV and flipped through the stations until she found a news channel that was reporting the incident. We all sat glued to our thirteen-inch black-and-white TV, listening as the morning news anchor recounted Dad's harrowing experience.

Apparently, Reed Williams—a convict at the Utah State Penitentiary—was being evaluated at the prison's mental health unit when he managed to break free and escape from the prison. First Williams stole a truck, then took a policeman hostage using the police officer's gun, handcuffs, and police car, and then, looking for another means of transportation, stole Dad's car and took him and Rhonda hostage. The reporter said that Dad, Rhonda, and the police officer were held captive the entire drive from St. George to Las Vegas and were eventually released.

"So when did Dad say he was going to call?" I asked Mom as soon as the news story was finished. "Are you sure he's okay?"

"Your dad is fine," she assured me. "And he said he would call tonight. Don't worry. He's okay."

I couldn't concentrate at school that day. All I could think about was Dad and his being held prisoner for hours by some crazy criminal who had a gun and could've shot him at any moment.

When Dad finally called that evening, I was a nervous wreck. The words that had been bottled up inside me poured out of my mouth the minute I started to speak.

"Are you okay, Dad? Is everything all right? Are you hurt? Where are you?"

"I'm fine," Dad assured me, though he didn't sound like his regular, confident self. He sounded upset and exhausted.

I peppered him with questions.

"So I know you were taken hostage but what exactly happened? How did you end up with that guy and how did you get away? Was he pointing his gun at you the whole time?"

Dad sighed and laughed a little. "So you want to know the whole story? Okay, I'll tell you."

Dad told me that four days earlier, he and Rhonda had driven to Los Angeles in an old Chevy station wagon he had recently picked up for three hundred dollars. He said they'd gone down to help a friend at a trade show and hoped to earn a few dollars selling tools, but after three days of working, they'd hardly made any sales and were discouraged and tired.

"The trade show wrapped up at 5 P.M. last night and that's around the time I called you." Dad explained. "I was exhausted and should have just stayed put for the evening, but I had promised to meet up with a sales guy in St. George the following morning and he had already purchased a motel room for us there, so we jumped in the car and started driving."

Dad said the drive took nearly six and a half hours. He was

so tired he could hardly keep his eyes open when he finally pulled into the Sand Dune Motel in St. George around midnight. He wanted to crawl into bed, but Rhonda had insisted on bringing her Chihuahua on the trip, and since the dog had been cooped up in the car for hours, Dad decided to take him for a quick walk and bathroom break so he wouldn't do anything on the motel room carpet. Dad said he was only back in the room for a minute or two before he heard a heavy knock on his door.

"I was too tired to be cautious so I opened the door a crack and saw a police officer. I tell you what, Ingrid. Before I could react, the door was forced open and the officer was pushed into my motel room. In the split second it took me to realize that the policeman was handcuffed and in the company of another man, I found myself staring down the barrel of a revolver.

"While my brain was trying to register what was happening, the gunman pushed his way in behind the police officer, shut the door, and started freaking out. He said, 'I'll blow your f'ing head off if you try anything!'"

Dad paused for a moment to let his words sink in. I felt my stomach cramping up. I could picture Dad opening the door, trying to figure out what a policeman was doing there, only to have some crazy man barge into his motel room with a gun, shove it in his face, and threaten to shoot him.

"The gunman looked young—I would say he was in his early to mid-twenties," Dad said, continuing his story. "He was pale and had a thin, wiry physique. And he was tall, really tall. I'd say he was around six foot six. He had this crazy look in his eyes and it was obvious he was high on something. He immediately demanded money and I tossed him my wallet, knowing full well it was empty. He flipped through it and came unglued when he realized there was no money in it.

"I tell you what, Ingrid. I thought I was a dead man for a minute. He started waving his gun around wildly and pointing it at my face. I knew I had to do something quick."

"So what did you do? Hadn't you already given him your wallet?"

"Well, I knew I had seventy-seven dollars in my front pocket, and I hoped I wouldn't have to give it up because it was all the money I had. But given his reaction, I decided he could have the money. I said, 'Wait, I think I have some money here,' grabbed it out of my shirt pocket, and tossed it on the bed in front of him.

"That seemed to appease him for a minute. He grabbed the money and then he asked if anyone else was in the room. That's when I thought about Rhonda. Before I could say anything, he pulled open the bathroom door and found her huddled on the floor in a corner next to the toilet.

"You know how Rhonda is, Ingrid. She's a homebody anyway and doesn't like excitement. Can you imagine how terrified she was?"

I could picture Rhonda cowering in the corner by the toilet, her body trembling as she listened to the gunman threatening to kill Dad, wondering if either of them would survive the night. It made me sad to think about.

Dad said the gunman ordered Rhonda to come out of the bathroom and sit down on the bed next to him and the police officer. Then he ordered Dad to turn over his car keys.

"I grabbed my key chain from my pocket, handed it to him,

and told him he could go ahead and take the car if he wanted. That's when he screamed for me to 'Shut up!'

"That's where I really started to get worried. Can you imagine what I was feeling? The gunman stared at all of us with his crazy eyes. He said, 'Now here's what we're going to do. All of you are going to quietly follow me outside and we are going to get into the car. If any one of you makes a sound or a stupid move, I'm going to blow your f'ing heads off.'

"I tell you what, Ingrid. My whole body was shaking as I led him to my car. He'd assumed that it was the shiny blue Cadillac parked in front of my room, and when we got to my car, which was parked a few doors down, I thought he was going to put an end to us right there. He was so angry he kicked the tires with his foot. 'This is yours?' he fumed. 'This is a piece of shit!'"

Dad and I both laughed when he told me this. I could picture the look of disgust on the gunman's face when he realized that Dad's beat-up station wagon was his getaway car.

"I think he realized right then that he had picked the wrong guy," Dad said, continuing to chuckle. "But at this point, there wasn't anything he could do about it."

Dad's voice got serious again as he went on with his story. He said the gunman opened the car doors and shoved the handcuffed officer into the front passenger seat. Then he ordered Dad and Rhonda into the backseat; Rhonda behind the police officer, Dad behind the driver's seat. He then handcuffed Dad's left hand to the passenger seat headrest and climbed behind the wheel. The gunman headed for the freeway and turned west, toward the desolate Nevada desert.

Dad watched the man's eyes dart repeatedly from the road to the rearview mirror.

"He was clearly nervous and started threatening us. He said, 'If I even see another police car, all of you are dead! Do you get that? You just better hope like hell I don't see a police car.'

"At this point, a voice in my head was screaming, 'You're in deep shit, Jerry. Deep shit!' You want to know the one thought that kept playing over and over in my mind, Ingrid? It was how grateful I was that I had called to say hello to you and the other kids earlier in the evening. That's all I could think about." Dad's call from the night before replayed in my mind. It was just a regular call. He and I talked for a few minutes like we always did, and Dad told me he would be coming for a visit in a few days. What if that had been the last time I ever talked with him or heard his voice? What if I never saw him again and was stuck with Earl indefinitely?

I couldn't bear to think of it and switched my attention back to Dad, who was continuing on with his story.

"About fifteen minutes into our drive, the gunman noticed that the car was low on gas and pulled off the freeway into a 7-Eleven to fill up. He grabbed Rhonda and yanked her out of the car, warning me and the police officer that he would blow her brains out if we tried anything. As soon as they were gone, the police officer filled me in on the events leading up to our being taken hostage."

Like the news report I had heard, Dad said the officer had told him that the gunman, Reed Williams, had escaped from the mental ward of the Utah State Penitentiary earlier that afternoon, where he had been taken for an evaluation. Williams immediately hot-wired a pickup truck and made his escape. Needing cash, he had tried to pawn the truck's toolbox off to the first man he came across. The man found Williams's behavior suspicious and called the police.

The police officer told Dad that when he and his partner were dispatched to check things out, they found themselves in a high-speed freeway chase that ended with Williams crashing the truck into the home of the police chief for Cedar City, a small town about forty miles north of St. George.

"He said he and his partner arrived on the scene and apprehended Williams, but as he was trying to handcuff him, Williams overpowered him, took his gun, and escaped the scene with him as his hostage. Just imagine it, Ingrid. He took the police officer hostage in his own squad car and drove off! Then Williams got onto the police radio and threatened to kill him if another police car came within sight.

"He told me Williams decided to ditch the police car in St. George and had just happened to pass the Sand Dune Inn when he spotted me walking the dog. He figured I was good for some money and another means of transportation. When he finished his story, he looked me square in the eye and said, 'He's going to kill us.'

"Before I could say anything, the gunman was back with Rhonda and shoved her into the backseat. I looked over at her, trying to catch her eye. But she wouldn't look up from her lap. That's when I noticed she was covered in hives."

Dad sounded sad when he said this and I wondered if he and Rhonda were even on speaking terms. Aside from the two weeks she had spent with us in Texas early in the summer, I knew

Rhonda and Dad had hardly spent any time together since they were married. Though I hadn't been around her much, I knew that she was the quiet, nervous type who preferred to stay at home. Dad had probably had to coax her pretty hard to get her to go on the trip with him to Los Angeles. I could see her in my mind, frozen in fear in her seat, covered in hives as she waited for the guy to flip out and kill her.

Dad continued with his story. "The gunman got back on the freeway, once again heading west toward the Nevada desert. He made constant threats. He'd say things like, 'My family kills people. My grandfather shot my grandma right through the head and then killed himself' or 'I don't have anything to lose by blasting a hole through all of your heads. You just better hope that I don't see a police car. If I even get a glimpse of one, I'm going to shoot a hole through all of your f'king heads!'

"By this point, I was struggling to come to terms with what I was sure was my impending death. I expected that any minute now, the guy would turn the car off onto one of the narrow dirt roads that headed into the vast, empty desert, shoot us, and leave our bodies there. I just kept thinking about you and the other kids, wondering how you would react to the news that your daddy had been taken hostage and murdered."

I was so upset by the thought of this that I couldn't speak. I just held the phone tight against my ear, waiting for Dad to continue with his story.

Dad said time seemed to expand and even stop. Every once in a while, he tried to catch Rhonda's eye, but she continued to stare into her lap. Then, about an hour and a half into the ride, Dad remembered that earlier in the day, he had tossed a large wrench into the backseat of the car after tightening a bolt on a loose battery wire.

"Right then and there, I knew there was hope. I worked my right hand into the crevice of the seat and locked my fingers around the long metal handle. I can't tell you the relief that rushed through me, Ingrid. The minute I touched the metal, I knew we were going to live. I knew that if I had to, I could take that wrench and slam it against the gunman's head. It wasn't something I wanted to do, because I didn't want his blood on my hands—plus I didn't want to get in trouble with the law for killing him. But I knew that if he turned off into the desert that was exactly what I was going to do. And I was going to finish the job because I wasn't going to take any chances."

Now that he knew they were going to make it out alive, Dad tried to catch Rhonda's eye again to give her silent assurance that everything was going to be okay. But he said she wouldn't look at him.

"Now that I was feeling more in control of the situation, I tried to engage Williams in positive conversation," Dad explained. "He seemed to calm down a little and eventually he started talking about Las Vegas. He asked me if I knew how to get to Caesar's Palace and I quickly assured him that I could get him there.

"I was trying not to let my optimism show but at this point, I was beginning to relax a little. I didn't think he would shoot us under the bright lights of Caesar's Palace, and the closer we got to the city and away from the desert, the less likely death seemed for either him or us."

At around 4 A.M., Dad said they reached Las Vegas and he

directed Williams to the parking lot behind Caesar's Palace. Without saying a word, Dad said Williams parked the car, got out, opened the passenger door where Dad was sitting, and redid the handcuffs so that he and Rhonda were cuffed together. He then opened the hood of the car and pulled out the battery cables and other wires so the car horn wouldn't work.

"He came back to the car and ordered us to stay inside. Then he took the car keys, shut the door and simply walked away, losing himself in the crowd and lights of Vegas. I can't even tell you what a wave of relief washed over me, Ingrid.

"We stayed seated for about five minutes to ensure he was gone. Then Rhonda slipped her small hand out of the handcuff and unlocked the doors. The three of us hurried to the security station in Caesar's Palace to report the incident.

"You want to know the real ironic thing about all of this?" Dad said, wrapping up his harrowing story. "The police officers at the police station treated me worse than the guy who took us hostage. Think about it, Ingrid. He's taken all of my money and ruined my car and we've just gone through hell for the last four hours. What do the police do? They interrogate us for six hours and then when they are finally done, they just tell us to go. They captured Williams at a bar within a couple of hours and had retrieved most of my money but they wouldn't give it to me; they told me they had to keep it for evidence. Rhonda and I were hungry, exhausted, and broke, but they didn't offer us any food or a place to sleep. If your uncle Dallas didn't live down here, I don't know what I would have done.

"At least I can understand where Williams was coming from," Dad added. "I can put myself in his desperate situation and think about what I would have done under those circumstances. But those police officers had no excuse."

Dad and I had been talking for nearly an hour and he said he was tired and needed to get some sleep. My head was spinning as I hung up the phone. I couldn't believe how close he had come to being killed. But that was too hard to process mentally so I shut it out of my mind and instead focused on Dad's amazing story. I was so proud of him for making it through the situation; I was certain part of it had to do with his incredible sales ability.

The next day, our local newspaper ran an article. Overnight, Dad became a local hero.

Mom was as excited as the rest of us were. She spread the front page of the newspaper across the kitchen table so we could all read it together. When we were finished, she retrieved a pair of scissors from her sewing room and began cutting out the article.

When Earl saw what she was doing, the blood vessels on the side of his face puffed up so big I thought they were going to burst.

"I think you need to remember who your husband is," he seethed at Mom. "And right now I'm hungry and need some breakfast."

Mom shot him an annoyed look. "I'll be there in a minute," she said quietly.

Earl glared at her.

"Well, just make it fast," he bellowed as he stomped out of the room.

I loved it that Mom wasn't putting up with his crap for once. I felt like high-fiving her.

I took the newspaper clipping to my social studies class that morning and shared the article as my current news event.

"My dad, Jerry Ricks, was taken hostage by an escaped prison convict," I started out, my voice full of pride. "But he managed to get free and everything's fine."

My classmates listened with awe as I recounted the story as Dad had told it to me. I even detected a little envy in their voices when they asked me questions. None of them had a parent who had been taken hostage. For the next few days, I was a celebrity at school.

13

. . .

Connie graduated from high school the same day I wrapped up ninth grade, and wasted no time making her escape.

She walked across the auditorium stage to receive her diploma, dropped by a few graduation parties to say her good-byes, and then headed home to pack. A week earlier, she had run a stop sign and crashed into another car, totaling the Honda that Dad had given her. But neither lack of transportation—nor the fact that Earl forbade Mom to help her by giving her a ride—was going to stop her from getting out of our house.

At eight o'clock the next morning, her friend Liz arrived in her Chevy Luv pickup to take Connie to her new life in Jackson, Wyoming, where she had signed on as a motel maid for the summer. A few days earlier, Liz had stood by Connie's side as she went through the wrenching agony of saying good-bye to her dog, Abbey, and finding a new home for her. Now, Liz helped my sister carry her suitcase and a couple of boxes of belongings out to the Chevy. Against Earl's orders, Mom ran out to say good-bye and snuck Liz some gas money. Then Liz and Connie drove away.

Connie's exit from my life didn't fully sink in because I was focused on my own escape. A few hours after her departure, Mom drove me to the airport to catch a plane to Dallas so I could be with Dad.

I had been counting down the hours until our reunion ever since my plane ticket had arrived in the mail the week before. The minute my plane parked at the gate, I elbowed my way into the aisle and impatiently waited for the throng of passengers in front of me to move. Relief washed over me as soon as I saw Dad.

"Hey, Dad!" I yelled, running into his open arms for a hug. "Finally!"

I wrapped my arms tight around his waist and breathed in his Old Spice aftershave. It felt so good to be with him that I didn't want to let go.

"How's my girl?" he asked, pulling away from me so he could take a good look. "I think you're getting more beautiful every time I see you. How is that possible?"

I felt calm and relaxed as we walked hand in hand to collect my suitcase at baggage claim and then headed to where Dad had parked. Every year his vehicle changed—this time it was a white van, which Dad had outfitted with shelves to organize his tool merchandise. I noticed a sleeping bag, pillow, and foam mattress stuffed in the back when Dad opened it to toss in my suitcase.

I climbed into the passenger seat, leaned back, and took a deep breath. I was free.

I didn't consider how Mom must have felt about losing two

daughters within a few hours of each other until the next day, when Dad called home to check in with the other kids. Instead of their usual bickering over child support, Mom confided to Dad that she had just had a fight with Earl and had become so angry she had thrown some of his things out onto the sidewalk.

"Why don't you just get rid of him?" I heard him say into the phone. "You know I never put you through this kind of misery."

When he hung up, he looked upset and I asked him what she had said. "She said she's trying to get rid of him, really trying."

I wanted to feel hopeful that Mom might actually follow through with her threat, but knowing Mom and the whole temple marriage situation, it didn't seem likely.

"Yeah, right," I muttered. "That's wishful thinking."

Dad and I spent our first few days together making the rounds to tool wholesalers in Dallas and Fort Worth to load up on merchandise. We also spent a couple of days with Rhonda, who had flown out for a quick visit. Since the hostage incident, she preferred to stay in Utah and Dad told me they rarely saw each other anymore. Within a week of my arrival, she was gone and Dad and I were back on the road selling.

Our life picked up where we'd left off nine months earlier, only this time Dad had a more organized sales crew who worked the highways alongside us and met up with us every night at a predesignated Motel 6 in one of the hundreds of towns that dotted the Midwest.

The guys in Dad's sales crew—whom I secretly nicknamed "the leech mobile"—seemed more interested in having a good time than actually making any money. I couldn't wait to get going in the morning so that we could get away from them.

Once on the road, I had Dad to myself for at least the next twelve hours.

Dad and I had a lot of downtime while driving around searching for prospects, and when we weren't kicking back listening to Kenny Rogers, Waylon Jennings, or other country singers crooning on the radio, we spent our time debating current issues, sharing dreams, and swapping stories about our lives.

Dad filled me with tales of growing up on a farm in rural northern Utah. His parents, Hazel and Joel, were just out of high school when they married. Grandpa Joel, who had grown up working on his parents' farm, had no money to purchase a home for himself and his teenage bride so they moved into a dilapidated, four-room shack situated on fifty acres of farmland that his parents owned. Dad spent the first few years of his life there, sharing the tiny space with his parents, his older sister, his younger brother, his uncle, his aunt, and their two kids.

"Our little shack didn't have any indoor plumbing or electricity, so when we needed water, your grandma would have to pump it from the backyard well—even when the snow was piled three feet high outside," Dad recalled as we drove the highway. "To keep us warm at night, your grandma would heat bricks in our coal-burning stove, wrap them in newspaper, and put them at the foot of our beds. Can you imagine having to do that, Ingrid? And every time one of us needed to use the restroom, we had to trek a hundred feet to the outhouse. I think that was the worst part. I was just a little boy and I was petrified of getting locked in there."

As the second child and first-born son in a family that would eventually swell to eleven children, Dad told me he had to start working as soon as he could understand what was being asked of him. By the time he was four, he was already helping Grandpa Joel milk the cows and make the rounds to feed the animals. And he said his workload skyrocketed just after his sixth birthday, when Grandpa Joel was forced to take on a second full-time job to support his growing family.

"My dad—your grandpa—got me out of bed at 4 A.M. every morning so we could make the two-hour rounds with the animals. Then he would drive the eight-mile journey to Logan and hop a bus for another fifty-mile ride to Ogden, where he worked a construction job. He couldn't make it back in time for the afternoon rounds with the animals, so that became my job. Every day after school, I raced home to feed the pigs, milk the cows, and clean the barn.

"I was good at math. I could do my times tables when I was four years old because my grandpa would always quiz me," Dad added. "But I wasn't a good student. I was always so tired from having to get up before the crack of dawn to milk the cows and take care of the animals that I sometimes fell asleep at my desk. Just imagine it, Ingrid. I was only six years old when I started doing that, and the work continued all the way through school. I know I could have done well at school. But I never had any time to do homework because as soon as I arrived home each day, I worked until it was time to eat. Then I was so tired I usually just went to sleep."

I felt bad for Dad when he told me these stories. I could imagine him as a little boy, having to work all the time and never having any time for fun. And I knew the pain he felt at never being able to join in with other kids to play arcade games or go to the movies. Dad told me he would go to scouting events sometimes but always had to cut out early when they went for an ice cream or a hamburger because he didn't have the money to cover it.

In the winter months, Dad said Grandpa was laid off from his construction job, forcing his family to survive on his forty-five dollar monthly unemployment check. For Dad and his brothers, this meant two pair of jeans and a pair of shoes to get them through the entire school year. "Your grandma tried to patch the holes as best as she could, but after a while, even the patches weren't enough. I was teased all the time and was constantly getting into fights at school because of it."

Dad shook his head and I could tell by the look on his face that the memory still upset him.

"Let me tell you something, Ingrid. I would read these books on slavery and about how slaves were given a run-down shack and a little food in exchange for their labor. Then I would look at my dad and realize he was a slave. He worked so hard every day and all he got in exchange was barely enough to put a shack over our heads and feed us. I decided that I was going to do whatever it took to escape that life."

Dad figured the first step to achieving greatness was to be the best at anything he did. If he was milking cows, he made sure his cows gave more milk than other cows around. If he was picking beans, he continued picking until he had out-picked everyone else around him.

"I wanted to prove to everyone I had what it took to be a winner," he explained. "Once, I went on a Boy Scout camping trip and decided that I was going to win one of the awards they were giving out. So while the other boys played, I stayed in my tent practicing slipknots over and over. And you know what, Ingrid? I won first place. That was a valuable lesson for me. I learned that if I put my mind to something, I could succeed."

Dad paused and his voice got hard.

"I tell you what really drove it home for me, Ingrid. One Sunday after milking cows, me and my brother Dallas changed into our nicest clothes—which weren't very nice—and starting walking the mile to church. We'd only gone a couple of blocks when a car slowed down beside us.

"The driver rolled down his window and said, 'Would you two boys like a ride?' I recognized the man and the woman who sat beside him as a couple from church, and eagerly accepted their offer. Dallas and I climbed into the backseat and sat quietly, silently congratulating ourselves on our good fortune. Maybe the woman didn't think we could hear her or maybe she meant for us to hear, but I will never forget those next few words. She glanced back at us, then turned to her husband and said in a loud whisper, 'Just look at those poor boys. Do you think they will ever amount to anything?'

"I tell you what, Ingrid. Her words cut through me like a sharp knife. My first reaction was to climb over the seat and slug her. Instead, I sat quietly and didn't say a word. But inside, I was burning. At that moment, I made a vow to myself. I said, 'Lady, I'll amount to ten times the person you are.'"

Dad's face turned red when he told the story and my heart ached for him. I finally understood why he was always working so hard to build a successful business. I also understood why he couldn't work for anyone else. He had been a slave the whole time he was growing up, and he was through being told what to do.

After graduating from high school, Dad said he left the farm and headed to Hollywood, where he joined a flight attendant school and hoped to land a career in the airline industry. When that didn't pan out, he headed back to Utah and since had nothing better to do, he decided he would do what boys his age were expected to do: go on a two-year Mormon mission. He figured it would give him time to think through what he wanted to do with his life.

Dad landed in Austria, a country he quickly fell in love with, and then quickly fell for Mom too.

"Your mom was so pretty back then, and I remember being impressed by how determined she was," Dad said, shaking his head at the memory. "I just didn't know she was going to turn into a dictator and slave driver. If she would have just accepted me for who I was, we wouldn't have had any problems."

I had seen pictures of Mom and Dad on their wedding day and had come across one of them hanging out on a beach in their swimming suits. They both looked young and happy and I thought they made a nice-looking couple. I agreed with Dad; Mom was very pretty back then. And I loved the stylish sixties clothing she wore. She looked like a completely different person in the pictures than the Mom I knew. She looked carefree and fun.

When it was my turn to talk, I mostly recounted Earl stories. Over the past year, he had taken his whole "head of the house-hold" act to a new level. Out of the blue, he decided that pants should only be worn by him and ordered Mom to wear dresses at all times. He also insisted that she grow out her hair and continued to make her wait on him hand and foot, even though she worked full time and he was self-employed.

Mom did her best to comply with all of Earl's demands. But when he started bringing home bags of frog legs and ordered her to fry them up for him, she refused.

"I'm sorry, but I can't do this," she said, staring in disgust at the pile of rubbery limbs. "This is something I just can't do."

"You'll learn to do what I tell you to do," he fumed as he grabbed the frying pan, filled it with vegetable oil, and dumped in a pile of the legs.

A few days later, he marched into the living room for our morning scriptures with a Bible he had bookmarked.

"You should've seen how much he was gloating," I fumed to Dad as we drove. "He flipped it open to the bookmarked page and started quoting some scripture about how God wanted women to obey their husbands. I thought Mom was going to explode. She didn't say anything, but she was twisting the corner of her skirt so tight while he lectured her that it looked like it was going to snap. And her eyes were on fire."

Though I didn't want to admit it to Dad or anyone else, I was scared of Earl. Everything about him was creepy, and I never knew what he was going to do next.

Once, I arrived home from school and headed to our enclosed back porch to get the laundry from our dryer when I noticed a weird smell and felt something dripping on me. I looked up and saw three furry, blood-soaked rabbit skins hanging from the clothesline Mom had strung up across the back porch for drying her nylons.

For a minute I was too frozen in fear to make a sound. Connie had three pet rabbits and I was certain I was staring at their remains.

My eyes locked on Mom's deep freezer five feet away. I moved toward it, flipped it open, and saw bloody gobs of flesh shoved inside gallon-size storage bags.

I heard footsteps and turned to see Earl standing behind me, a cruel grin plastered on his face. His grease-stained hands were covered in blood. "Just wait until you taste it," Earl said with a sneer, stepping closer toward me. "You're going to love it."

There was no way anything he killed was getting anywhere near my mouth, but Earl had such a crazy look in his eye, I didn't dare challenge him.

"I have to do my homework," I mumbled, pushing my way past him. I bolted to my room and hid until Mom came home from work. As soon as I heard the front door open, I ran down to greet her. Earl was right behind me.

"Hey, Mom, can I talk with you for a minute?" I pleaded. "Alone?"

Earl didn't let Mom answer.

"Anything you need to say to your mom you can say to me too," he said, stepping between the two of us.

"Please, Mom. Just for a few minutes."

"Did you hear what I said!" Earl barked. "If you want to say something to your mom, you're saying it to me too!"

Mom looked at Earl and back at me. She didn't speak for a minute.

"I've had a long day and I'm tired," she said finally. "I'm going to rest for a minute and then I need to make dinner."

Earl flashed me a victory grin and then trailed behind Mom into the kitchen.

Mom never said anything about the bloody mess dangling from her clothesline, but she must have put her foot down with Earl because that night at dinner, she served spaghetti while Earl sawed into the undercooked blob of meat on his plate.

The next day, when Earl was off on a rare errand, I ran out to the edge of our half-acre backyard and saw that Connie's rabbits were still there and still alive. Mom must have watched me because when I came back into the house, she tried to explain away Earl's creepy behavior by blaming it on the emotional trauma he had experienced while fighting in Vietnam.

I didn't really care what made him a psycho creep. What I cared about was that Mom actually let this man come into our house and make our lives miserable. Until Earl, I didn't know I was capable of hating anyone so much, and any association with him was more than I could stand.

When the church telephone directory arrived with my name attributed to his, I used Wite-Out to erase it and then wrote in my own last name over the top of it. When the mail came, I would gingerly sort through it with the top of my fingers and then carefully pick out the family mail—leaving his in the mailbox so I wouldn't have to touch it.

Not long after the rabbit incident, I was walking by Mom's bedroom and noticed Earl's briefcase open on their bed. Taped to one side of it was an 8 x 10 picture of the group wedding shot Mom had forced us all to pose for.

A hot rage shot through me. For a minute, I considered ripping the picture into tiny shreds. Then I saw the blue ink pen lying next to it. I grabbed it and scribbled out the image of my face, pushing so hard I nearly poked a hole through it.

I was in the kitchen doing dishes that evening when I heard Mom's voice yelling for me to come into the living room. I knew from the tone of her voice that something was wrong, and it wasn't hard to guess what it was.

I took a deep breath, trying to calm myself as I walked down the hallway and rounded the corner.

She was standing in the center of the room. Earl hovered over her, clutching the picture in his left hand.

"Did you do this?" Mom asked, spitting out her words as she motioned toward the picture. "Did you?"

Any hope I had that she would listen to my side of the story vanished. I glared at Earl, who looked like he'd just won the lottery.

Mom's hand flew at my face, slapping it so hard I could feel her fingerprints pressing in on my cheek even after her hand had left it. She swung back and hit me again. My face was stinging. But it was nothing compared to the hurt going on inside me.

Mom had never hit anyone in the face. Ever. She had always taught us that it was the worst thing a person could do to another person. But she had done it to me—and on his behalf.

She might as well have ripped out my heart.

I glanced at Earl, whose grin was stretched so big and tight across his face I hoped it would snap in half. Then I looked at Mom and stared her straight in the eye so she could see what she had just done.

I held it together until I made it up the splintered wooden stairs to my attic room and shoved my nightstand up against the door as a barricade. Then I grabbed my pillow from my bed, buried my still-stinging face into it, and let the sobs come.

Despite what I considered to be the ultimate betrayal by Mom, I still considered her a safety net because Earl seemed to know there was a line he couldn't cross when Mom was there. When she wasn't there, all bets were off.

To avoid being alone with him, I usually made sure I always had someplace to be after school. Sometimes I had volleyball practice or a game.

But most of the time, I headed to Mr. Tabbot's room—where I had been going for more than a year. Mr. Tabbot, my art teacher from eighth grade, was a tall, lanky man who never raised his voice or said a mean word to anyone. One day after art class, he asked me to stay behind for a minute.

"You know I'm always here after school for an hour or so preparing for the next day," he said gently. "Any time you want, you're welcome to come hang out."

From that day on, I became a regular in his class after school. We never talked much. Usually I would just do my homework while he was prepping for the next day. But I felt peaceful and safe while I was there. I hung out in his room until it was time to catch the activity bus, which put me home just after Mom.

The tension had gotten so thick between Earl and me that I knew better than to be alone with him. Once, not long after the Family Home Evening incident, I wasn't feeling well and had decided to take the regular bus home from school.

Earl must have watched me step off the school bus at the top of our block, because when I walked through the door and rounded the corner, he was waiting for me.

He grabbed my arm, forcing me to drop my backpack.

For a minute, I was too scared to make a sound. He was so close I could feel his hot, smelly breath on my neck, and when I looked down, I saw a black leather belt in his free hand.

"I'm going to show you who rules this house now!" he sneered, dragging me by my arm into his bedroom.

"Let go of me!" I screamed, praying in my head that my neighbors could hear. "Get away from me! Somebody help!"

Earl shoved me face first down on the bed and slammed the belt against my back. Before he could whip me a second time, I flipped my body around so I was facing him and began kicking and thrashing wildly.

"Get AWAY from me!" I screamed again, hoping my voice would carry through the thick brick walls.

Earl tried to grab hold of me again but I kicked him in the stomach and caught him off guard. That was all I needed to break free of his grasp. I tore out of the room, swung open the door to the attic, and sprinted up the stairs. As soon as I made it into my room, I slammed my door shut, sat down, and pushed my body hard against it—extending my legs against my bed to act as a brace.

I was terrified that he would come up after me and bust through the door. But he never came. He must have been worried that someone had heard my screams, or that Mom was going to come home.

After I finished telling Dad this last story, he didn't speak for several long minutes. His hands were gripping the steering wheel so tight it looked like the circulation was gone from them.

"So what did your mom do?" he asked finally.

"Nothing," I answered bitterly. "I didn't even tell her because I know she doesn't want to hear it. She probably wouldn't have believed me anyway. It's like she's not even there anymore."

Dad was silent for a minute more before he spoke.

"Maybe I ought to just go there and kill Earl, and get rid of him once and for all."

His eyes were hard and dark.

"What in the hell is your mom thinking?" he added, talking more to himself than me. "We had our problems, but you know I never treated her or any of you kids like that. She thought she was doing a good thing by getting rid of me. All she did was make the worst mistake of her life."

Dad sometimes used our time on the road to educate me on what he felt were the most important lessons in life. He taught me about the functions of a car engine and had me recite the parts of an engine to him from front to back. He also spent what seemed like endless hours talking about the one-track mind of boys and the need to stay clear of them at all costs. He warned me never to get drunk with a member of the opposite sex, telling me that if a boy could get me drunk, he could get me to do anything. He worried about me throwing my life away by getting involved with a boy, and sometimes used trick questions to test me.

"Would you have sex with a guy for a million dollars?" he asked me once.

I hesitated.

"Would you have sex with a guy for ten dollars?"

"No, of course not!" I replied, shooting him a dirty look.

"Well, we've already determined what you are," Dad returned evenly. "Now we're just negotiating a price."

I didn't know how to respond to this. He had a point. On the other hand, a million dollars was a million dollars. And Dad and I both dreamed of being rich. In fact, Dad was obsessed with it.

Ever since I could remember, Dad had talked about building a million-dollar business and had explored lots of business opportunities trying to strike gold. Before becoming a traveling salesman, he had owned a gas station, a hot dog shop, a taxicab company, and a janitorial business. He had also participated in and launched numerous multilevel marketing companies. Nothing had worked so far, but Dad was determined to succeed.

At least once a week, he repeated his mantra.

"Ingrid, your daddy's going to be a millionaire someday. What do you think of that?" To keep ourselves pumped up, Dad and I had a standing weekly date with the television series *Dallas*. Dad loved J.R., the main character, because he was a savvy, ruthless businessman who had millions of dollars, and also because Dad's name, Jerry Ricks, shared the same initials.

"You know what time it is, don't you?" Dad would say each Friday night, a few minutes before the show was to begin.

"It's *Dallas* time," I would yell back.

If we were at a motel, we kicked back on our beds, each with a can of Sugar Free Dr Pepper, and flipped on the TV. If we were spending the night in the van, we found a truck stop lounge, plopped down on one of the couches, and lost ourselves in the lives of J.R., Sue Ellen, and the rest of the *Dallas* gang.

Dad was determined to become as successful as J.R., and it was fun to fantasize about our life once he had finally built his multimillion dollar company and had so much money he couldn't spend it all if he tried. Dad would still work, of course. He loved to work and would go crazy if he sat around doing nothing. But with all that money, he'd be able to afford a fancy Cadillac and a big motor home that he would travel in and use as his base instead of the old, worn-out vehicles that were constantly breaking down on us.

I decided the first thing I would do is go shopping for a house of my own. I no longer cared about being whisked away by the Osmonds, but I still had a recurring daydream about a big, beautiful house. I used to envision Connie living there with me, but now that she was gone, I decided I would invite Heidi. The house would be situated in Logan so I could still see my friends and go to the same school, but it would be located on the hill where the rich people lived. And it would be far enough away from Earl that I'd never have to see him again.

I believed in Dad and was convinced he could reach his million-dollar goal if he could just become a little more savvy and ruthless like his role model on *Dallas* and learn to say "no" to the leeches that always sucked him dry.

It took only one look at the three or four guys who made up Dad's revolving sales crew to know that they weren't our ticket to success. They were a disgusting combination of bad teeth, stringy hair, and tight jeans—and looked and smelled like they hadn't showered in weeks. They all either smoked or chewed tobacco and often stood outside their motel rooms polluting the air with their cigarettes or spitting out mouthfuls of black tar onto the sidewalk.

I could barely stand to look at them, but I still could've tolerated them if they'd carried their weight. After all, the whole idea of having them on the road with us was to generate more revenue for Dad. Each night, we met for dinner at a predesignated Denny's or some other motel cafe to map out our plan for the next day. Dad would settle up with the guys—supplying them with tools on consignment as needed and collecting money for the tools they had sold. In theory, Dad was supposed to receive a ten percent commission in exchange for supplying the tools. But it never worked out that way. Half the time, the guys didn't sell anything at all and Dad would have to pay for their dinner and then give them gas money for the next day.

When I asked why he was covering their costs when they were supposed to be paying us, he acted like it was just part of doing business.

"Oh, Ingrid, sometimes you just need to have a little patience," he said. "They just need a little help to get them going and then it will start to pay off."

Dad couldn't believe that anyone would purposely try to rip him off or take advantage of him, and was always giving the guys second, third, even fourth chances.

A couple years earlier, when he was still running his tool company out of Salt Lake City, he told me that one of his sales guys had taken off with a semitruck loaded with merchandise. Dad had reported it to the police, who tracked the guy down and arrested him. The sales guy used the one call he was allowed to phone Dad and plead his case. And Dad ended up going down and getting him released from jail.

Being a Good Samaritan was one thing, but helping someone get out of jail after they had just stolen from you was taking it too far.

"So why did you do it?" I asked, trying not to sound as irritated as I felt. "I know I wouldn't have."

I could tell by the sound of Dad's voice that I had hurt his feelings.

"Well, for one thing, I knew he would be grateful and wouldn't steal from me again," Dad said defensively. "But I also know that everyone deserves a second chance. Wouldn't you want a second chance, Ingrid?"

Most nights, we were done with the guys after dinner, and I didn't have to see them again until the following night. But sometimes, if they had a particularly bad sales day, Dad would invite them to stay in our motel room with us so they wouldn't have to spring for a room themselves.

This meant giving up my bed. For privacy, I would take the bedspread off Dad's bed, grab one of his pillows, and create a makeshift bed on the floor in the small space between Dad's bed and the wall.

I hated giving up my bed. But the worst part was sharing the bathroom with them. I always made sure I was the first one in the bathroom each evening so I wouldn't have to put up with the smell the room emitted later. In the morning, I always flushed the toilet and washed off the seat with a washcloth before I sat down.

I had been putting up with the occasional sales crew sleepover for a few weeks and hadn't said a word. But when Dad told me one evening after dinner that we were giving up our motel room to one of his sales guys because he had a girlfriend with him, I'd had enough.

"But what about us?" I asked, growing angrier by the second. "We worked hard to earn the money for that room. Where are we even going to clean up?"

Normally I wouldn't have minded sleeping in the van, but I was furious that Dad was so willing to sacrifice my comfort for some woman we didn't even know. What's more, when we did spend the night in the van, we always slept at a rest area or truck stop so I had easy access to a bathroom and could clean up in the morning.

Dad looked at me like there was something wrong with me.

"Ingrid, what did you expect me to do?" he asked, exasperated. "They didn't have any money. They needed a place to stay."

I spent the night seething as I tossed and turned on the foam mattress that separated Dad and me from the van's hard metal floor. My jeans were tight and uncomfortable. I had to use the restroom but didn't dare knock on the door in the middle of the night. Finally, at five in the morning, I couldn't stand it any longer. I fumbled in the dark for the latch to the van door and climbed out. I walked up to the motel room door and pounded on it.

After what seemed like an eternity, the girlfriend—wrapped in a sheet—answered the door. She didn't say a word. She just shot me an annoyed look.

"I need to use the restroom," I mumbled as I pushed my way past her. The woman climbed back into bed and was already asleep when I passed through the room a few minutes later and headed back to the van to start my workday.

"It's just how it goes," Dad said as we drove to a nearby 7-Eleven to gas up and grab a Sugar Free Dr Pepper. "They needed our room more than we did last night. Someday I'm sure you'll understand."

14

. . .

Even during my time with Dad, I had been looking forward to fall because I was finally going to be in high school. But the minute I walked into the house and Dad drove away, the pit in my stomach was back and the same crushing depression—like being trapped between two stone walls that were closing in on me—took hold. Only now Connie wasn't around to help push the walls back.

When Dad called the next evening to check in, I sobbed into the phone, so choked up I could barely speak.

"What's the matter, Ingrid?" he asked, his voice cracking. "Talk to me. What's wrong?"

I couldn't explain the emotions colliding inside me; the knots in my stomach and the way I had lain in bed the night before, fighting off waves of panic that washed over me. Or the suffocating air that filled the house and the hopelessness that wrapped around me like a straitjacket. But my desperation must have sounded through my sobs.

"We are getting you out of there," Dad announced flatly before hanging up.

Within a few minutes, first my grandma, then an aunt who lived near Salt Lake City called—both offering to let me live with them. Connie, who had finished the summer in Jackson and was now in Southern Utah getting ready to attend her first quarter of college, also called and offered to let me come live in her tiny one-bedroom apartment.

Dad was doing his best to find a solution for me. The problem with all of these offers was that I wouldn't be able to attend high school with my friends. I didn't want to leave them and start new in a strange place.

Something had changed in Mom over the summer. After three years of living through Earl's daily tirades and threats, she suddenly seemed to understand the devastating toll it was taking on our family. And despite feeling trapped in her marriage to Earl, she was as determined as Dad to help find a better living situation for me.

That evening she invited me to go for a walk so we could figure out a place for me to live.

For a few minutes we both walked in silence. I focused on the dairy processing plant that loomed in front of us, remembering how when we were little, Connie and I used to race each other on our bikes from our house to the plant. Sometimes, when we got home, the ice cream truck would be making its way down the street and Mom usually managed to scrounge together enough change for us each to pick something.

"I talked with Sister Perry and she says you can live with her," Mom said finally, her voice barely audible.

I knew she was just trying to help, but this was the last thing I wanted. The woman was as religious as Mom and even stricter—she didn't even let her daughter wear makeup.

I wanted to scream at Mom, to demand that she throw Earl out and do something to start fixing our family instead of acting so powerless to it all. I also wanted to hug her to try to heal her broken heart, and thank her for her willingness to help me.

I stayed quiet and kept walking. Mom was quiet too.

After a while, she reached for my hand and took it in hers. It felt good to be near her. This was the first time we'd spent an uninterrupted hour together since she and Earl had married. I didn't realize until then how much I had missed her.

"I have an idea," Mom said after a half hour of silence, a hint of hope in her voice. "Why don't we go talk to the bishop about it and see what he thinks you should do?"

Normally I would have scoffed at the idea. As far as I could tell, it was Mom's constant discussions with a bishop that had brought on this whole mess in the first place. But at the moment, I was feeling so conflicted I didn't know what else to do. And I really liked our new bishop. He was a firefighter by profession and had warm, kind eyes. Even Dad liked him.

As soon as we got back to the house, Mom called and made an emergency appointment. Thirty minutes later, we were sitting in Bishop Whitten's living room.

"Can I get you two a glass of water or something?" he asked before taking a seat.

Bishop Whitten was about six feet tall with black hair and clear blue eyes that seemed to look right into your soul. I knew his daughter from my church classes and had always been a little envious that he was her dad. He was constantly taking her skiing or doing other fun things with her, and seemed so nice and caring.

"So why don't you tell me what's going on?" he asked kindly, nodding toward me.

I wanted to speak but I was too torn up inside and didn't trust myself to talk. So Mom did the talking.

Bishop Whitten waited until she was finished and then turned his attention to me.

"From what I'm hearing, it definitely sounds like you shouldn't be living in the same house as Earl," he said. I detected empathy and even concern in his voice.

"Maybe you can live with your grandma so you can still be close by. That seems like the best solution to me."

I left his house grateful that he understood my situation, but just as conflicted as before. Out of all my options, I liked the idea of living with Grandma the best. But the truth was that I hardly even knew Grandma. Before my parents were divorced, Mom used to take all of us out to Grandma's house for a Sunday visit a couple times a month. But usually Connie and I just played games in her TV room while Mom and Grandma were visiting. And after Mom married Earl, we only saw her once or twice a year.

Grandma always remembered us with cards on our birthdays. But with eleven children of her own, she had so many grandchildren to keep track of it was hard for her to maintain close relationships with any of them.

I spent the evening considering the Grandma option. She was easygoing and I knew it would be peaceful living with her. But she lived seven miles outside the city limits, which meant I would have to go to a different high school. And since I was too young for my driver's license and had no way of getting around, it also meant I would spend most of my time stuck on a farm in the middle of nowhere.

I went to sleep still undecided. The next morning, as I tried to block out our morning scriptures, my eyes locked on Earl. He shot me an ugly, victorious grin.

My gut burned as the realization slowly washed over me. I was playing into his hands. All he needed was for me to be completely out of the picture and there would be no one to stop him—or at least try to stand in his way.

He had already started referring to himself as Daniel's "daddy" whenever I was in earshot, and just before leaving with Dad for the summer, I caught him spanking Daniel and berating him because he didn't say his prayer. I had hurried to find Mom, desperate for her to intervene. But she just sat frozen on the living room couch, listening as my brother cried. I knew Heidi, who had just turned thirteen, was too sick with her asthma to put up a fight. And my brothers were too young to defend themselves. That moment of clarity made me understand I couldn't leave.

"I think I'll give it a try here for a couple of weeks," I told Dad when he called to check in that evening.

"Are you sure, Ingrid? Are you sure that's what you want to do?" He sounded both surprised and suspicious.

"Yeah, I'm sure, Dad. I think everything's going to be fine. I'll explain it all later."

I looked over at Earl, who was standing a few feet away,

listening to my side of the conversation. I saw the angry, dumb-founded look on his face. I stared into his icy, mean eyes and flashed him my biggest smile.

I loved high school. It was so much bigger and freer than junior high, and I could choose from all sorts of classes and after-school activities. Mom insisted that I go to seminary—a Mormon religion class that had its own building adjacent to the high school campus. But aside from that, she didn't care what classes I took; so while my friends' parents made sure they were enrolled in AP classes, I signed up for the easiest math and English classes available. Unlike junior high, the high school was only four blocks from my house, making it possible for me to stay at school as long as I wanted after classes ended each day without worrying about how I was going to get home.

My new strategy at home—in addition to staying away as much as possible—was to pretend like Earl didn't exist; and it seemed to be working. Though Mom and I never discussed it, my decision to stick it out at home came with an unspoken agreement between us that from that point on, only she had a say in my life. I didn't know it at the time, but Bishop Whitten had also stepped in on my behalf. He had met with Mom and Earl and told them that Earl should stick to being a husband, stop trying to play any sort of father role, and leave me alone.

So that I could earn some spending money, Mom lined up a weekly housecleaning job for me with one of her patients and gave me a ride to her home each Saturday. The rest of my free time was spent with my new friend, Heather, who had instantly become my soul mate.

I had been without a best friend since the end of seventh grade, when Phyllis had decided to quit the Mormon's Indian Student Placement Program and stayed on the reservation with her real family. I'd known Heather from a couple of classes we'd had together in junior high, but our friendship didn't click until we partnered up in biology class.

Just the idea of dissecting frogs made me light-headed. But Heather—who didn't shy away from anything—was fine with it.

"Don't worry about it, I'll do all the cutting," she assured me. "You can just stand by and watch."

Heather was everything I wanted to be. She was slim and beautiful, with dark brown hair, sea-blue eyes, and a perfect soprano singing voice. Even though she was only a sophomore, she had already landed a role in our high school musical. She was also one of the most headstrong people I knew. I avoided confrontation whenever possible, but Heather had no problem arguing with anyone. And she was good at it.

Heather was the youngest of four children and was the only one of her siblings left at home. I loved going to her house because it was peaceful. It was also the kind of house I had always wanted. It was a modern ranch style with nice furnishings, new carpet, and three bathrooms—all with their own showers.

I was embarrassed to have friends over to my house, and I knew some girls at school avoided me because I was poor. But Heather didn't care about where I lived or how much money my mom had. And her parents quickly accepted me despite my whole broken-family situation.

Heather's dad was an engineering professor at the university. I also knew from Heather that he was in the stake presidency, which was an even higher ranking than bishop, and that worried me a little. But he only asked me once if my dad was a priesthood holder. When I answered with a curt "No," he never brought the subject up again. Instead, he asked me questions about what I wanted to do with my life and focused on correcting my grammar.

"It's not 'me and Heather,'" he would prod in a kind, teacher sort of way as he drove us to a movie or the arcade. "It's 'Heather and I.'"

Soon I became a regular fixture at Heather's house after school and on the weekends. And when I walked in, her mother always greeted me with a smile.

"Well, hi there, Ingrid," she would say, either looking up from the magazine she was reading or from the homemade dish she was preparing for dinner. "Would either of you like a snack?"

Between my Saturday cleaning job, hanging out with Heather, and the occasional dates I was now being asked out on, I was rarely home anymore and the school year flew by.

Though I didn't see Mom much, I knew she was exhausted from her long hours at the Health Department and her ongoing, nightmarish struggle with Earl. But I didn't ask about it because it seemed pointless.

"You know what I was thinking?" she asked quietly one Saturday in March as she drove me to my weekly cleaning job. "I was thinking of taking a vacation with just you kids this summer. That way we can all get a break from Earl and spend some time as a family."

I heard the wistfulness in her voice and it made me sad. A family vacation without Earl sounded fun—a vacation at all sounded fun. We hadn't been on a vacation since before the Mississippi move.

But I knew there was no way Earl would let her go off on her own. And as much as she was dreaming of an escape, I knew she knew it too.

I wondered if she was feeling out the waters to see if maybe I would stay around for the summer, given that the school year had gone so much better than years before. But that was out of the question. Summers belonged to Dad and me.

"Sounds nice, Mom," I said after a while, reaching over to squeeze her hand. "You and the kids deserve a break from Earl. I hope you get it."

Next to my friendship with Heather, the best thing about my first year in high school was turning sixteen. Along with being allowed to date, I was finally eligible to get my driver's license—which I hoped meant that I would soon be getting a car from Dad.

Though my birthday was in January, the soonest I could take the mandatory driver's education course was in the spring. During occasional visits home from college, Connie gave me driving lessons and I managed to get my driver's license two days before flying to Wichita, Kansas, to start another summer with Dad.

"Do you have your license yet?" he asked as soon as I met him at the airport gate.

"Yup, just got it," I answered, proudly taking it out of my wallet.

"Well, that's great news! How would you like to drive a car to Iowa tomorrow?"

"Really?"

Dad laughed. "Really. You remember my buddy Harold, don't you? He needs the car and this would be the easiest way to get it to him.

"By the way, I've got a car surprise waiting for you too," he added, a grin breaking across his face. "You don't think I forgot about you, did you?"

I thought I was going to crawl out of my skin with excitement. "Are you serious? Thank you, Dad! What is it?"

"You want to be surprised, don't you?"

I looked at Dad with an excited, pleading look.

"Okay. I'll give you a hint. It's a 1974 Volkswagen Super Beetle and it's the cutest thing you've ever seen. But it's got a bad engine at the moment. I've got it sitting in a parking lot in Fort Worth. But I'll promise you something right now, Ingrid. Before the summer's over, I'm going to have it fixed so we can drive it back home. What do you think of that?"

I was on such a sudden high, I thought I might float away. "Are you kidding? I love Volkswagen Bugs!" I nearly shouted, throwing my arms around him for a hug. "Thank you, Dad. Thank you, thank you, thank you!"

"I figured that would put you in a good mood." Dad chuckled and shook his head. "The next time we're in Texas stocking up on tools, I'll take you to see it. But right now we've got to get Harold the car I owe him. Are you ready to get to it?"

"Definitely!" I replied, my thoughts still on the VW Bug waiting for me in Texas. I couldn't wait to see it. And I couldn't wait to get it home. It meant Heather and I would finally have our own transportation instead of depending on her parents to give us rides.

We climbed into Dad's van and drove from the airport directly to a warehouse parking lot where a rusty, mustard-colored Ford Pinto sat waiting. I grabbed the keys from him, opened the door, and climbed in.

That's when I spied the stick shift.

My heart sank. I didn't know how to drive a stick shift. I barely knew how to drive an automatic.

I explained this deal-breaking news to Dad, but he wasn't even slightly deterred.

"Oh, Ingrid, driving a stick shift isn't that hard. You can think, right? It's really pretty simple. I'll just teach you."

Dad climbed into the passenger seat beside me while I adjusted the seat so I could reach the pedals.

He immediately began instructing me.

"Now, you see that pedal next to the brake?" he said, pointing to a pad on the floor.

I nodded my head.

"That's called the clutch. Just remember that if you don't push that in when you try to shift, nothing is going to happen."

I spent the next hour driving the car around the parking lot, with Dad coaching me on when to push in the clutch, shift the gear, and hit the gas pedal.

"See, there's nothing to it," he said as I made my practice

loops around the lot. "I knew you would be fine. Now that you've got the hang of it here, let's try the highway."

"Are you sure I'm ready for that?" I asked, looking at the cars whizzing by on the four-lane freeway that sat adjacent to the parking lot.

"Of course you're ready," Dad replied. "You're my Hippie Boy, aren't you? Besides, I'm going to be right there with you, coaching you all the way through it."

Somehow I managed to make it through the ten-mile highway loop without stalling the car or crashing into another vehicle. But that was with Dad sitting next to me, yelling out instructions every five seconds. The idea of navigating the car on my own through two states' worth of freeways sounded like suicide.

"I'm really not sure this is such a good idea, Dad," I said when we were finally back safe in the parking lot. "I mean, I did just get my driver's license. Maybe we should spend a few more days practicing."

Dad looked at me like I had a screw loose.

"That's nonsense. You just have to remember what I'm teaching you and use your head a little. We'll leave early, before any traffic is on the road. Once you get going on the freeway, you'll be fine."

I wasn't sure I agreed with his assessment. In fact, I was pretty certain I was going to get into a wreck the following day. But I didn't say any more because I didn't want Dad to think I was a wimp.

The next morning, we checked out of our motel and climbed into our separate vehicles. Dad told me to follow close behind his van and to pull over to the side of the road if I saw him flash his taillights.

"Ready for an adventure, Ingrid?" he asked through my open car window.

"Sure," I replied, forcing my voice to sound confident.

"All right. Let's get to it then. We've got a lot of miles to cover."

Dad walked back to his van and hopped into the driver's seat. A minute later his lights went on and he pulled out of the dark motel parking lot. I followed him through several sets of traffic lights without problems. But then we hit the highway on-ramp.

Somewhere between remembering to accelerate on the gas, push in the clutch, and shift gears, all while trying to keep my eyes on the road in front of me, I forgot about the need to get the car up to speed before merging into traffic. As a result, I pulled onto the highway going about twenty miles an hour, causing the car behind me to swerve over into the left lane to avoid hitting me. Luckily, there were no other vehicles on the road and the car sped off into the darkness.

Dad immediately flashed his taillights. I followed his van to the apron on the highway and turned off the ignition.

He came running toward me, his face the reddish purple color it always turned before he exploded.

"What in the hell are you doing?" he screamed. "Push on the gas! You've got to keep accelerating! We're on the highway now. What are you trying to do? Get yourself killed?"

"Sorry, Dad," I mumbled, feeling my own anger creeping through me. "I'm doing my best."

"Well your best needs to get a whole lot better than that or we're not going to make it."

Dad stood by my car window for a moment, trying to decide what to do next. I didn't want to disappoint him, but I was so freaked out about the idea of driving another five hundred miles on the freeway that I hoped he would say he'd changed his mind.

"Everything's going to be fine, Ingrid," he said finally, his voice back to being calm. "You just need to pay attention and think and you'll be okay."

With that, he turned and walked back to his van.

I took a deep breath, turned on the ignition, and waited for Dad's van to move in front of me. "Clutch, shift, gas. Clutch, shift, gas," I repeated as I picked up speed and made my way back onto the road.

It wasn't the smoothest ride, but I managed to shift at the appropriate times and get the car up to sixty miles an hour and in fourth gear—what Dad called "cruising speed." Once the first hour was behind me, I relaxed a little and started to enjoy the ride. I turned the radio knob to an oldies station and sang along to Beatles songs as I drove.

I had always felt free driving in the passenger's seat with Dad. But that was nothing compared to the freedom I was now experiencing. My thoughts drifted to my Volkswagen Beetle waiting for me in Fort Worth. I couldn't believe I was going to have a car of my own. I couldn't wait to get behind the wheel and go.

By the time Dad flashed his turn signal four hours later and waved his hand out the window, motioning me to get into the far right lane and exit the freeway, I felt like I had been driving a stick shift for years.

We pulled into a McDonald's and headed inside for a bite to eat.

"See, Ingrid, I told you it's a piece of cake," Dad said as we bit into our sausage egg McMuffins. "You just have to believe in yourself."

We finished eating, filled up our gas tanks, and hit the road again. By midafternoon we made it to Des Moines and headed straight for Harold's house, a small, white, wood-framed house located in a city neighborhood.

Harold was a big, jolly guy and I always thought he would play a great Santa Claus. He was self-employed like Dad, and over the years the two of them had worked several business deals together. Mostly, though, they were just good friends. Dad used Harold's house as a base to receive mail and messages, and he sometimes crashed there when he was passing through town.

Harold waddled out to greet us as soon as we pulled up in front of his house.

"Well, look at you," he said, his eyes scanning over me as I climbed out of the Pinto and handed him the car keys. "How did you get to be driving age?"

I felt myself blushing. "Just happened, I guess."

We spent the evening visiting with Harold and crashed in our van overnight. The next day, Dad told Harold the van had been giving him mechanical problems so the three of us went to a used car lot and traded it in for a forest-green, wood-paneled Plymouth station wagon. Then Dad and I were on our way.

"So where are your sales guys working?" I asked as soon we

were back on the highway. "Are we planning to hook up with them like last year?"

Just the mention of them made Dad's face turn red.

"Let me tell you something about those guys, Ingrid. They were all a bunch of worthless crooks who used me and stole from me. I left one of them in charge at the office in Texas and let me tell you, what a mistake that was. I had signed some blank checks before I left and told him he could cash them once I had money in the bank. You know what he did? He filled them out for a total of ten thousand dollars, cashed them at a bank, and took off. And now, because it was my signature on the checks, there's a warrant out for my arrest."

I spun around to face him, my heart suddenly pounding a million beats a minute.

"A warrant for your arrest? Seriously? Dad, what are you going to do?" My concern snapped Dad out of his bad mood.

"Oh, don't worry about that," he said, laughing as he spoke. "You know I got the golden tongue, Ingrid. Nobody's going to do nothing to me. Plus, I didn't do anything wrong. I'm just telling you the story so you know what a bunch of crooks I was dealing with. But they're gone. And now that I've got my real sales partner back, we're going to be back on top in no time."

I had to bite my tongue. If Dad had just listened to me a year ago, I could have saved him a lot of trouble.

"Well, I'm glad you're rid of them," I said, trying to force myself to sound positive. "And you're right, I'm the only sales crew you need."

Dad and I spent the next few weeks working throughout

Oklahoma, Kansas, and Iowa. We still had a few wrenches, screwdrivers, and metric socket sets we were pushing, but most of our inventory consisted of hydraulic jacks.

Dad told me that he had hooked up with the hydraulic jack supplier in the spring and at first thought it was going to become his ticket to success. The jacks were compact and sold for only fifty dollars, but were supposed to be strong enough to prop up a semitruck. Dad knew this was a lie, though, because he'd tried out one of the jacks on his van and it had busted.

"I've got to decide what I'm going to do," he said as we drove along looking for prospects. "If a guy buys one of these jacks and it breaks on him, he could get hurt and I don't want that on my conscience. But I've got a lot of money tied up in these jacks so I've got to figure out how to get rid of them."

After discussing it, Dad concluded that the thing to do was liquidate the jacks we had, then head up to a sales meeting that Joe, the hydraulic jack supplier, was holding in Madison, Wisconsin, in a week or so to discuss the situation with him. Maybe he had better quality jacks he could sell to Dad.

We decided to map out a work route that would land us in Madison in time for the meeting. Since joining up with Dad the month before, we had been alternating nights between rest areas and Motel 6s to save money, but a couple of days into our work trip to Wisconsin, Dad decided we deserved to splurge a little.

"How about you and me get a room at a Holiday Inn and just relax for the evening," he said midafternoon as we pulled into Davenport, Iowa. "We can kick back and order room service. What do you think about that?"

"Sounds great to me," I replied with a smile. Better eight years late than never, I was tempted to say.

We checked into the Holiday Inn around 4 P.M., carried our boxes of tools into the room, and kicked back on our beds to relax. Just because I could, I made sure to order a cheeseburger and French fries from the room service menu.

Around seven that evening, the phone rang. Dad and I looked at each other in surprise. No one knew we were staying at the motel. Who could possibly be calling us?

"It's probably just the wrong room number," Dad said as he picked up the phone.

Within seconds of saying hello, a smile broke across his face. "Well, this is a surprise. How in the world did you find me here?"

I watched Dad as he talked, curious about the person on the other end.

Whoever it was, he was clearly enjoying the conversation, and I could tell by the way he cooed into the phone that it was a woman.

Dad asked how the person on the other end of the phone line was doing and spent a lot of the conversation smiling and listening.

"Well, we've got to get to Wisconsin in a couple of days for a meeting, but maybe after that we'll come out that way and see you," Dad said as he wrapped up the phone conversation. "It'd be great for you to meet my daughter. I think you two would really hit it off."

"Who was that?" I asked as soon as he hung up the phone. Dad smiled and shook his head.

"I can't believe it," he said finally, a goofy smile plastered on his face. "That was Debbie, a woman I met a few months ago in Amarillo. She asked me at the time where I lived and I told her Holiday Inn, USA."

"But how did she know where we were staying? I mean, we never stay at a Holiday Inn. And there must be hundreds of them across the country."

"That's what's so remarkable," Dad said, still wearing the same goofy grin. "She told me she just kept calling all of the Holiday Inns throughout the Midwest every night until she found me."

"Wow, that's some serious determination." And a little creepy and desperate, I thought to myself. Who would spend hours every night for months trying to track down a man she had met a couple of times?

Dad filled in the story for me. He explained that back in April, he'd been selling tools near Amarillo, Texas, with a member of his now-disbanded sales crew. As a reward for a great sales day, Dad had taken the guy out to a country-western bar in town. When Dad walked into the bar, he noticed a table full of women laughing and decided to join in the fun.

"I started asking them one by one to dance," Dad said. "When I started dancing with Debbie, we began talking and I thought she was really pleasant and enjoyable. She told me she works as a telephone operator for AT&T, so I thought I would mess with her mind a little."

"So what did you do?" I asked, seeing the mischievous spark in Dad's eye.

"I looked at her and said, 'You want me to let you in on a little secret? I get my long distance for free.' She looked at me like she didn't believe me. She said, 'And just how do you do that?' So I told her how I sometimes make long distance calls at pay phones and then tell the operator to bill the call to some business I pick out of the phone book."

Dad chuckled at the memory. "She looked at me for a minute and shook her head. Then she said, 'Well, that's not right.' I could hear the disapproval in her voice, but I think she was also a little impressed and we really hit it off. I danced with her a few more times and even took her to a movie the next day before heading out of town. But that was three months ago, and I didn't expect to ever see or talk to her again."

I could picture some desperate lady, sitting at home, calling one motel after another trying to locate Dad. That had to be expensive. But then again, Dad said she was a telephone operator so maybe she got a discount. Clearly she had too much time on her hands.

"Wow, Dad, she must really like you," I teased, amused that he was so happy to hear from her.

Had it been the year before, I would have been jealous that some woman was trying to cut into my time with Dad. But now that I had dated a few times myself, I thought it was great that someone was interested in him. I often worried about Dad being on the road alone while I was in school. Though he was still married to Rhonda, they hadn't seen or contacted each other in more than a year, and I knew their relationship was over.

"Oh, Debbie's just a friend," Dad replied, the grin still plastered on his face. "And she's really young. She's twenty-two. Think about it, Ingrid. That makes her exactly half my age."

There was no wiping the smile off of Dad's face. I couldn't remember ever seeing him this giddy.

"I guess you're right, Ingrid. It does sound like she has a crush on me."

He chuckled and shook his head again. "Yeah, I would say she's hooked. But then again, who can resist your daddy?"

15

. . .

It was still dark when I stumbled into the rest stop bathroom to brush my teeth and get ready for the day.

I splashed cold water on my face and pulled out my Neutrogena face soap that I kept carefully wrapped in a thin, white cotton washcloth I had taken from a Motel 6. The soap was critical when I was traveling with Dad because, between the heat and the junk food, my face was prone to breakouts and the soap was the only thing that kept my skin smooth and clear.

I spent the next few minutes brushing the tangles from my shoulder-length hair and applying a quick coat of mascara, trying to make myself out in the blur of metal on the wall. Then I headed into the handicap toilet stall to change into a fresh pair of shorts and a clean tank top. It was 5 A.M. and time to hit the road if Dad and I wanted to make it to Wisconsin at a decent hour.

By the time I returned to the station wagon, Dad had already put away our pillows and sleeping bags.

"You took so long I could have slept for another half hour. Are you all cleaned up and beautiful now?" he said as I slid into the passenger seat beside him.

I loved early summer mornings in the Midwest—the way the sun came up out of the ground and seemed to sit on the fields before creeping into the sky. I loved the crisp, cool air and the quietness around us as we drove. Aside from the occasional semitruck, there were no other vehicles in sight. It was like the freeway was a never-ending open road built just for Dad and me.

I breathed in the air and smiled, excited about the day ahead. Dad and I had decided to take the day off from work because, aside from two jacks, we had sold out of all our tools. Dad wanted to be refreshed and relaxed when he got to his meeting that evening so he could confront Joe about the faulty hydraulic jacks he'd been selling us.

I'd never been to Madison and couldn't wait to get there. Dad told me it was a fun town and said if we got there early enough, we would celebrate by renting another room at a Holiday Inn and spending a few hours relaxing before the meeting.

We were in southern Illinois, just a little more than two hundred miles away, which meant we could get there in time for a late breakfast and have the entire day to ourselves if we hustled.

"So what do you think, Ingrid?" Dad asked, patting my leg.

"I think everything's great," I said, rolling down my window so I could feel the early morning air rush against my face.

We sped down the freeway, pushing the Plymouth as fast as it would go. Dad turned on the radio and scanned the selections.

He stopped on a country station. As if we had planned it, Willie's Nelson's "On the Road Again" started playing.

Dad turned the volume as loud as it would go and we both began belting out the lyrics. We knew the song by heart. It was like Willie Nelson had written it with us in mind. I tilted my head back against the headrest and hung my arm out the window as we sang, soaking in the moment. This was already turning into a great day.

We were midway through the last chorus when Dad abruptly turned off the radio. I sat up in my seat and looked over at him. His face was tight and his smile was gone.

"What's wrong, Dad? What's going on?"

He didn't answer. But his eyes darted to the rearview mirror. I turned toward the back windshield to see what he was looking at and saw red flashing lights closing in on us. Dad eased up on the gas pedal and steered the car over to the shoulder of the road.

"What in the hell was I thinking?" he muttered as he turned off the ignition switch.

I watched the highway patrolman walk toward our car. He was at least six feet tall with thick arms and a broad build that reminded me of a heavyweight boxer. He wore a brown ranger hat that matched his uniform and had on reflective sunglasses that made it impossible to see his eyes.

Dad rolled down his window.

"How you doin', Officer?" he asked, flashing a warm smile.

"Do you know how fast you were going?" the patrolman asked.

"I know I was going a little fast," Dad said in an apologetic tone. "We were just trying to get to Wisconsin for a meeting and there were no cars on the road so I guess I wasn't really paying attention."

"Seventy-five miles an hour. That's twenty miles over the speed limit."

"Was I really going that fast? I'm sorry, Officer. I didn't realize it." Dad was smiling and trying to act congenial but I could tell he was nervous. He gripped the steering wheel with both hands and his knuckles were turning white.

"Let me see your driver's license and registration."

Dad pulled his wallet from his back pocket, fumbled for his driver's license, and handed it to the scowling patrolman.

"Ingrid, will you look in there and see if you can find the registration for me?" he asked, motioning toward the glove compartment.

I opened it and frantically began shoving around the mass of papers, knowing intuitively that I wasn't going to find it.

Dad turned back to the patrolman.

"I guess I'm not really sure where the registration is, but the car is registered and we definitely have insurance." Dad offered him another sincere, apologetic smile.

"Stay put," the officer said. "I'll be back in a minute."

Dad watched in the rearview mirror as the patrolman walked back to his car. His hands were still on the steering wheel and I noticed that his right hand was shaking. I had never seen him scared before, and it was scaring me.

My mind flashed back to our conversation about the arrest warrant in Texas because of the checks his ex-sales guy had bounced. Once Dad explained it, it hadn't seemed like a big deal to me. He liked to refer to himself as a "creative financier" and often floated checks to get through tough times. He always eventually paid back any checks that bounced. And this time it wasn't even him who had done the bouncing.

At least five minutes lapsed. Dad didn't speak; he just kept glancing at the rearview mirror.

"Oh shit!" he yelled suddenly. His face had turned chalk-colored. Before I could respond, I saw the patrolman at Dad's door. Then I saw his gun, pointed only a few inches from Dad's head.

"Get your arms in the air and keep your hands where I can see them! And don't make any sudden moves!"

We both threw up our arms and kept our bodies frozen. I was too scared to breathe. The cop yanked the car door open with one hand while keeping the gun trained on Dad. He grabbed Dad by his left arm, yanked him out of the car, and pulled him around to the back, where he threw him against the back of the station wagon.

I stayed frozen in my seat, watching in what seemed like slow motion as he slammed Dad against the trunk a second time and pulled out handcuffs, which he clamped down on Dad's wrists. I felt tears streaming down my face and heard a strange howling noise coming from inside me.

Dad lay bent over the car, his face smashed against the steel. The patrolman frisked him and pulled his wallet from his back pocket. He spent a minute combing through our tool money, about one thousand three hundred dollars—mostly in tens and twenties.

"Looks like a lot of money to be carrying around on you," the patrolman said.

"What's this?" he asked seconds later, pulling out an ID card from Dad's wallet.

"Jerry Jones, huh? What other names do you go by?"

"I had that made up as a joke," I heard Dad say, his face still smashed against the car.

"Shut up!" the officer snarled.

I watched as he pushed Dad toward his patrol car and locked him in the backseat. Then he was at my window.

"How old are you?" he asked.

"Sixteen."

"Let me see your driver's license."

I couldn't stop my hand from trembling as I reached for the card. Mascara streamed down the front of my face and smeared as I wiped my eyes.

The officer grabbed it out of my hand. He stared hard and then laughed.

"Are you sure this is you?" he sneered as he tossed it back into my lap.

"So you live in Utah?" he continued, motioning toward my driver's license.

I nodded my head.

"Do you have a way to get back there?"

"No," I managed between sobs.

"Well, we're probably going to end up extraditing your dad to Texas so I don't know what we're going to do with you."

He paused for a moment. He frowned, and then spoke.

"Normally we would impound the car, but since you can drive, here's what I want you to do. I want you to follow me back to the police station and we can figure out what to do with you from there."

A fresh round of sobs had taken over and I was crying too hard to speak. I nodded my head again in response.

"Sure you're in a condition to drive?" he asked.

Another nod.

The patrolman walked back to his car. I crawled over into Dad's seat and adjusted it forward as far as it would go. Then I turned the key in the ignition and pulled out behind the squad car. I glanced at the car clock. It read 5:40 A.M.

I kept my eyes trained on the taillights in front of me, unable to stop crying. The patrolman's words played over and over in my head.

Your dad will probably be extradited to Texas, and if he is, I don't know what we are going to do with you.

I felt dizzy and too overwhelmed to try to sort through it all. Tight, sharp cramps filled my stomach. I kept thinking of Dad smashed against the trunk and the handcuffs and the way the patrolman shoved him into the back of the squad car. What was going to happen to us?

We stayed on the freeway for about twenty minutes before exiting and turning into the town of Tampico, Illinois. A large banner with the words "Birthplace of Ronald Reagan" hung across the empty main street.

I followed the squad car into a large, vacant parking lot. The patrolman stepped out of his vehicle and motioned for me to stop.

He walked over to my window. "You can leave the car here for now and come with me," he said.

I watched him pull Dad out of the car by his arms and followed the two of them across the street to the county jail. We headed into a small room where the sheriff sat leaning back in his chair, waiting to take a look at his prize capture. He reminded me of an overweight bulldog. His broad nose was squished flat against his fat face and he had squinty eyes that were partly covered by thick, droopy eyelids. His gut spilled into his lap and pressed against the buttons on his mud-brown shirt, leaving a gap just above his belly. I wanted to take his badge and stick him with it to wipe the smirk off his face.

The sheriff looked at Dad, glanced at me, and then turned to the patrolman, who still wore his reflective sunglasses even though the room was dark and windowless.

"What are we going to do with her?" the sheriff asked, nodding in my direction.

He and the patrolman talked it over for a minute and decided to call Mom to make sure I hadn't been kidnapped.

"I'm *not* kidnapped," I said, furious that they even suggested such a thing.

"We'll see about that," the sheriff said. "What's your mom's name and phone number?"

The last thing I needed was for them to call Mom. But the sheriff just glared at me until I told him her name and phone number.

I watched him punch the numbers into the phone pad with his stubby fingers. I could hear the phone ring four times through the phone receiver before Mom answered.

"I'm sorry to bother you, ma'am," he said, "but we're just here with your daughter, Ingrid. Jerry Ricks has been arrested and we're just trying to figure out what the situation is."

After talking with Mom for a few minutes, apparently convinced that I had a right to be with Dad, the sheriff handed me the phone.

"Hi, Mom," I said reluctantly.

I could hear Earl breathing hard, listening to the conversation from the other extension. I wanted to scream for him to get off the phone, that this wasn't any of his business.

"What's going on?" Mom asked.

I could hear concern and frustration in her voice. I knew she was silently accusing Dad of trouble and I could visualize the self-satisfied smirk on Earl's face.

"I'm fine. Everything's fine!" I yelled into the phone. My hand shook as I handed the receiver back to the sheriff.

He hung up the phone and looked at me for a minute without saying anything.

"Well," he said finally, "you are a minor, which means we could put you in foster care. But you're old enough to look out for yourself, and I'm not yet sure what's going to happen to your dad so I don't want to do anything premature."

I sucked in some air and stayed frozen, waiting for this man to decide my fate.

"But I'll tell you this much. If we end up extraditing your dad to Texas, we're going to have to find a foster home for you until you can figure out how to get back to Utah."

While the sheriff talked, Dad sat silently on a metal folding chair in the corner. Whenever I glanced over at him, he forced his lips into a smile.

I wanted to smile back, but I couldn't. I knew he was pretending. And seeing him sitting there in handcuffs and knowing they were about take him away from me and lock him up in some dingy cell had me so rattled and torn up inside I could barely breathe.

"Well, why don't you go get him booked," the sheriff said to the patrolman, who had yet to remove his sunglasses.

"I still don't know what we're going to do with you," the sheriff added, turning toward me. "Minors aren't allowed inside the county jail."

Dad spoke up. "Ingrid, why don't you just get a motel room and relax for a while?"

He had given me his wallet when we arrived inside the county jail, and the cash was still intact.

"That's a good idea," the sheriff agreed, looking relieved. "Just give us a call to let us know where you're at, and we'll keep you informed."

I bit my lip to keep from screaming as I watched the patrolman take Dad away. I waited until they were gone before approaching the sheriff. "I'm not getting a motel room," I said, shooting him a look that dared him to challenge me. "I'm not going anywhere without my dad. I'll just wait in the car."

He stared back at me and shrugged his shoulders. "Suit yourself. But it might be a long wait."

I was crying again when I left the county jail and headed back across the street to the parking lot. It was only 6:45 in the morning, but already the air was hot. I climbed into the car and rested my forehead on the steering wheel, wailing. I didn't want to get cheated out of my summer with Dad. Without school as a buffer, I couldn't stomach going back home to Mom and Earl. But I certainly didn't want to get stuck in a foster home. I needed

Dad, and I was petrified for him. What if they sent him to Texas? Would he end up going to jail for a long time? There was no way Dad could survive behind bars. He needed his freedom. He'd go crazy.

I wondered what was going through his mind. I pictured him alone in a dark, dirty cell—wildly pacing back and forth. Dad couldn't stand to be confined.

My head felt foggy and my stomach was churning. Maybe I just needed to eat something. I grabbed Dad's wallet, thick with our tool money, and walked a long block up the hill, where I found an Arby's. I choked down a breakfast sandwich and then ran to the bathroom to throw it up.

I didn't know when I might hear something about Dad, so I hurried back to the car to wait. My head was spinning. Panic shot through me whenever I allowed myself to think about what might happen, so I tried to shut it out of my mind.

Loneliness swallowed me. I needed someone to talk to and to be with me. I pulled out the orange notebook I still used to record our tool sales and started to write a letter to Heather, telling her about the awful situation. I sobbed as I scribbled down the words. When I finished the letter, I crumpled it up and threw it on the floor.

It was now 8 A.M. and already the temperature on the bank sign down the street read ninety-five degrees. It was even hotter inside the car. Beads of sweat ran down my forehead, and my legs stuck to the vinyl seat. I didn't care. I was glad I felt as miserable on the outside as I did on the inside. Without Dad, nothing mattered.

I cried until the tears wouldn't come anymore and then walked back to Arby's so I could use the restroom again. My stomach was in knots and I had terrible diarrhea. When I finished, I bought a Sugar Free Dr Pepper and headed back to the car to figure out what to do. I decided my first task was to find Dad.

I crossed the street and circled the county jailhouse, trying to peek into the foot-wide basement windows. I just needed to see him to make sure he was okay, and then talk to him so I could decide what to do. He would tell me the next step.

The windows were barred and it was so dark inside I couldn't see anything. After about a half hour, I returned to the car to wait.

Time stood still. I turned on the radio and flipped through the stations. Nothing was on. I turned it off, leaned back, and closed my eyes.

A rapping sound on the car window woke me, and I jumped in my seat. A police officer I hadn't seen before was standing there. I rubbed my eyes and rolled down the window.

"Hi," he said, his eyes taking in my matted, sweaty hair and puffy eyes. The guy looked young; I guessed that he was in his mid-twenties. His voice sounded kind—the first kindness I had heard all day.

"I have a letter from your dad. He asked if I would deliver it to you."

"Okay, thanks," I said, grabbing it out of his hands.

I waited until he left before unfolding the paper, which looked as if it had been ripped out of a school notebook. My hands were trembling so hard I had a difficult time reading Dad's words.

Ingrid,

They are talking about extraditing me to Texas, and you are my only hope. They might let me out if I can come up with the money I owe the bank. I need $10,000. I'm including a list of people for you to call to ask for money. But wait until you hear from me again before you do anything.

Love,
Dad

Listed below his signature were the names and phone numbers of several relatives and friends. Even Mom's name was on the list.

I felt like throwing up again as I read over the names. I couldn't call these people begging for money—particularly when I knew that everyone on the list was struggling just to pay bills and buy groceries. I could just imagine how Mom would react, given that Dad hadn't paid her the child support he owed her.

I glanced at the car clock. 10:30 A.M. I wondered if this day would ever end. Then again, maybe it was better if time didn't pass. I didn't know if I could handle what the future was going to bring.

I sat glued to the car seat, waiting for more news. I didn't dare leave because I worried that Dad would try to send me another message and I would miss it. The temperature had climbed to one hundred and one degrees. My tank top was now drenched and sticking to my back. I turned on the radio again, hoping to distract myself with music. I flipped through all of the AM stations, then made a run through FM, finally settling on country music. I drummed my fingers on the steering wheel for a few minutes, and then pulled out my journal and wrote a couple paragraphs about my day. I glanced at the clock. 12:05 P.M.

I had the windows rolled down, but the heat was making me sleepy and I didn't want anyone breaking into the car while I dosed. So I rolled them all up, leaving only an inch crack in each. Then I closed my eyes and tried to leave the day behind.

The knocking on my window startled me out of my sleep. I looked up to see the same police officer who had delivered the note from Dad. I quickly rolled down the window.

"Just wanted to let you know that we're taking your dad to a court hearing in about fifteen minutes," he told me. "You can come if you want. The courthouse is just a couple of blocks up the hill."

"Great. Thanks."

I knew I looked a mess but I didn't care. Once again, I waited for him to leave. Then I rubbed my eyes, grabbed my purse—which now contained Dad's wallet along with my brush and lip gloss—and jumped out of the car. I sprinted up the hill to the Arby's and glanced at the clock on the wall. It was 1:30 P.M.

I spent the next ten minutes in the bathroom. I splashed cold water on my face and used toilet paper and hand soap to clean the smeared mascara off my face. Then I brushed my teeth and repeatedly ran the hand dryer in an attempt to dry out my sweat-drenched tank top.

I walked back outside just in time to see a line of men in orange jumpsuits slowly making their way up the hill. Their hands were cuffed behind them and they were all connected together by a long chain that wrapped around each of their waists. I scanned the line until I found Dad.

He stared straight ahead as he walked and seemed to be having trouble keeping in sync with the other guys. I watched as he bumped into the man in front of him, then quickly stepped back and shook his head as if in apology. Compared to my slight, five foot two frame, Dad had always seemed big to me. But his five foot nine stature looked small and insignificant compared to the two men he was sandwiched between. Fresh tears began streaming down my face. I had to do something to save him.

When I arrived at the courthouse, the police officer who had told me about the hearing directed me to sit in the back left section of the courtroom. I saw Dad seated on the right side, in the front of the room with the rest of the guys in the orange jumpsuits.

"Everybody rise," a man said.

The judge, a stern-looking man who appeared to be in his early sixties, entered the room.

He immediately started going through the cases. As the case numbers were called out, the defendants were ordered one by one to stand in front of him. The judge briefly listened to the charges being levied against them and then decided whether to release them on bail or have them held without bond. Finally the judge called Dad's case number.

Dad stood up and took his place in front of him. The judge listened as the patrolman who had arrested Dad told him about the warrant in Texas on embezzlement charges.

"Well, it looks like he should be extradited to Texas," the judge announced after the officer had finished talking.

I felt like I had just been scalded with a branding iron. This couldn't be happening.

"No!" I yelled from my seat in the back of the room.

Everyone in the courtroom was suddenly staring at me. The judge looked bewildered.

"Who is this girl?"

"She's my daughter," Dad said quietly. The judge motioned in my direction.

"Why don't you come up here," he said kindly.

I made my way down the center aisle toward Dad, ignoring the whispers and stares. I clutched my purse in my left hand and grabbed Dad's hand with the other.

"How old are you?" the judge asked.

"Sixteen," I said between sobs.

He turned to the patrolman.

"Can you please explain what's going on here?"

The patrolman, who had finally removed his reflective sunglasses, told the judge that I had been with Dad at the time of his arrest and had been waiting in the car throughout the day for word of Dad's fate.

"Let me make sure I heard you right. You said you left her alone all day sitting in a blazing hot car?" The judge glared into the patrolman's beady eyes. "Is this how you would like your daughter to be treated?"

The patrolman didn't answer. I felt a twinge of hope. I shifted my purse so I could cross my fingers.

The judge shook his head in disgust and then turned to face Dad.

"Do you know how lucky you are to have a daughter who loves you so much?"

"Yes, I do, Your Honor." Dad's tone was somber and deferential. The judge contemplated the situation for a couple of minutes.

"I am ordering that you be released on a five thousand dollar fugitive bond," he said finally.

Dad squeezed my hand and I felt a rush of relief wash over me.

I looked back at the judge. He smiled down at me for a brief moment and I felt tears running down my face again, but this time they were tears of happiness.

"Thank you, Your Honor," Dad and I said in unison.

I glanced over at the patrolman. He looked like he'd been punched. I flashed him a smile and then rushed back to my seat to wait through the remaining proceedings. Dad was still in police custody so he walked back to the county jail with the other defendants. With the rebuke from the judge still fresh in his mind, the patrolman made sure to escort me back down the hill and told me I could wait in the administrative area of the county jail until Dad gathered the necessary funds. At first, I thought that we would have to come up with the full five thousand dollar bond and I assumed Dad was standing at a pay phone, making collect calls to the people on the list.

About an hour later, though, the same police officer who had delivered Dad's letter and told me about the hearing came out to where I was waiting. He said a bail bondsman would put up ninety percent of the bail. Following his instructions, I counted out five hundred dollars from Dad's wallet and slid it through a slot to the administrative clerk, who was stationed behind a thick, bulletproof window. Another twenty minutes passed and then Dad walked into the room where I was waiting. He was back in his jeans and button-down striped shirt. I glanced at the clock on the wall. 4:45 P.M.

"Let's go, Ingrid," he said, motioning toward the door.

Neither of us spoke as we vacated Ronald Reagan's birthplace. But as soon as we were back on the freeway, Dad let out a laugh.

"Well, Ingrid, that was a close one," he said, shaking his head.

I waited for him to thank me for saving him from jail or at least ask me how I had survived the day. Instead, he turned on the radio and started flipping through the stations as if nothing had happened.

I turned toward my window so he wouldn't see the humiliation and hurt on my face. I was suddenly embarrassed by my swollen eyes, which were still stinging from all the crying I had done. A familiar voice inside me was screaming, berating me for needing and loving him so much.

"Yeah, that was a close one," I said, the music drowning out my words. Then I closed my eyes so Dad would think I was asleep.

16

. . .

While the fugitive bond we paid in Illinois got Dad out of his jam there, he was still required to check in at the Fort Worth court-house within thirty days and pay another twenty-five hundred dollars in bail or sit in jail until his hearing in October.

His meeting with his hydraulic jack supplier had ended in a screaming match and Dad said he was finished dealing with him. But now we were without merchandise and had less than seven hundred dollars to purchase more inventory. Even worse, Dad wasn't sure what he wanted to sell. Jacks were out and no one seemed to be interested in wrenches or socket sets anymore.

We spent a day driving in silence toward Texas without a game plan. Dad wasn't speaking because he was too stressed out about the prospect of jail and how to come up with the bail money to avoid it, and I wasn't in the mood to talk because I was still nursing wounds from his arrest.

I couldn't stop from replaying the day in my mind. In those

long seconds when the patrolman pointed his gun at us, pulled Dad out of our car, and took him away from me, everything had changed.

Dad had stopped being the person who was always going to save me. He had become the person who needed to be saved.

It had all been way too close for comfort. What if I hadn't screamed out, "No!" from the back of the courtroom? What if the judge hadn't felt sorry for me? Dad would still be locked up in a cage, waiting to be transferred to another cage in Fort Worth. I would essentially be locked up in some stranger's house until Mom scraped together the money to get me back to Utah. And then I would be stuck at home with Earl for the summer—which was unthinkable.

It still stung that Dad didn't ask a single word about how I had managed to make it through the day while he was in jail. Was he even concerned about what I had been through? And would it kill him to acknowledge that it was because of my quick thinking that he was free?

I wanted to talk about it, to hear him describe what his day in jail had been like. I also wanted him to ask me about my day so I could tell him how I had stood up to that sheriff and had refused to leave the county jail vicinity without having Dad with me. I wanted to explain how I had circled the county jail building, searching for him, and how I had holed myself up in that car all day waiting and worrying. I wanted to tell him how it had ripped my heart out when I had seen him walking up that hill in the orange jumpsuit, chained to the other inmates. Most of all, I wanted to hear him say how proud he was of me for interrupting the courtroom proceedings and keeping that judge from shipping him off to a Texas jail.

We spent the night sleeping in the station wagon to save money. The next morning, about an hour into our still-aimless drive toward Texas, Dad announced that he was going to call his old friend JD for help. JD, like Dad, was a hotheaded, stubborn, charismatic, self-employed salesman who dabbled in anything he could get his hands on. When I was in fourth grade, JD and his longtime girlfriend, Kerrie, had set up a jewelry business in Logan. Some days after school, Connie and I headed over to their rental house and spent the afternoon stringing necklaces and bracelets, for which we received a dime each. Then JD and Kerrie took the items to arts and crafts shows, set up a booth, and passed our work off as authentic turquoise jewelry made by Navajo Indians.

JD and Dad drove each other crazy but when one of them was down, the other could usually be counted on for a lift. As it stood, Dad figured JD owed him a favor because a few years back, Dad had raised ten thousand dollars to get him out of a jam.

I waited in the car while he made his call to JD from a pay phone. I crossed my fingers, hoping the conversation would go well. I could tell just by looking at Dad that the pressure was getting to him. His face was pale and his mouth looked like it had been tattooed into a permanent frown. He had hardly eaten anything in the past two days. I may have been able to get him out of the jam in Illinois, but I had no clue how to miraculously make twenty-five hundred dollars appear so Dad could stay out of jail in Fort Worth. He needed someone to help him, and JD sounded like his only hope.

Dad stayed on the phone for twenty minutes and then hopped into the car. I couldn't tell by the look on his face how things had gone. I waited for him to speak.

"Well, Ingrid," he said finally. "Looks like we are heading to Austin. JD's selling ceiling fans there right now and said he would help."

I uncrossed my fingers and inhaled, feeling the relief wash over me.

"That's great, Dad." I reached over and patted his leg like he always did to me. He stared at the road ahead of us and shook his head, like he was trying to wake himself up from a bad dream.

"Yeah, I guess so. You know I hate asking people for help— even if they do owe me."

We landed in Austin, Texas, a day later and camped out at Kerrie and JD's house. I didn't want to get in Dad's way so I helped Kerrie sell some of her fake Navajo Indian jewelry at a nearby swap meet each day while he and JD hit the streets selling ceiling fans. In less than two weeks, Dad had the twenty-five hundred dollars we needed.

He decided we should head straight to Fort Worth so he could pay the bail and be done with it. He still wasn't sure what we were going to do for a living and was back to being silent. I knew not to bug him when he was in a mood like this so I kept silent too, hoping the cloud would pass.

"You thirsty?" he asked about an hour into the drive.

"Yeah."

"Me too. Let's take a little break."

Dad pulled off at the next exit and stopped at a small convenience store. I grabbed Sugar Free Dr Peppers for both of us and set them on the counter, where Dad was waiting to pay. By the time we got back to the car, his mood had shifted.

"Did you see all of those T-shirts and sunglasses in there?" he asked as he turned the key in the ignition.

"Yeah, I saw them," I replied, pulling back the tab on my drink.

"You know what I'm thinking, Ingrid? I think I'm going to start selling some of that."

I glanced at Dad. He was smiling and drumming his right hand against the steering wheel. It was like someone had flipped on a light switch inside of him. His mood had suddenly jumped.

"Just think, Ingrid. Can you imagine how many little mom-and-pop c-stores there are? There are thousands of them. Every town is full of them. And the owners are all looking for a way to make more money. I can get those T-shirts, glasses, videos— all that junk—for next to nothing."

"I think it sounds like a great idea," I offered, catching his enthusiasm. "I'll bet it would be pretty easy, too." In my mind, it sounded a lot easier than hunting down loners who looked like they had some money they wanted to part with.

"Yup, Ingrid. I've made a decision. I'm going into the trinket business."

As soon as we got to Fort Worth, Dad drove to the courthouse to make his mandatory appearance and pay bail. I waited in the station wagon and fed the parking meter with quarters during the hour he was gone.

When he returned, we headed to the wholesale district and spent the next two hours picking out sunglasses, cotton-polyester T-shirts, and an assortment of videos.

"Yeah, Ingrid, I definitely think this is our answer," he said as we loaded the boxes of merchandise into the back of the car.

Back in our seats, Dad rolled down the windows to let some air circulate through the hot car and turned on the radio. He turned left out of the parking lot and started driving down the city's back roads. I didn't ask where we were headed next. I was just glad things were back on track. I nestled into my seat, closed my eyes, and let the country music wash over me.

About ten minutes into the drive, Dad flipped off the radio. I opened my eyes and glanced over at him. A mischievous grin was painted on his face.

"How would you like to go check out that car of yours, Ingrid?"

His words caught me completely off guard. Of course I'd thought about the car the minute Dad said we would be heading toward Fort Worth. And I had spent at least an hour fantasizing about the car nearly every day since I had landed in Wichita and Dad had told me about it. But after everything that had happened in the past couple of weeks, I figured the car was the last thing on Dad's mind, and I didn't dare ask about it.

"Are you serious? Really?"

"Of course I'm serious. You didn't think I had forgotten about it, did you?" Dad laughed and shook his head. "Sometimes I don't know about you, Ingrid."

All of the stress and hurt and anger from the past two weeks melted away in an instant. Dad had remembered his promise about the car.

My heart raced as we headed to another wholesale warehouse

where Dad sometimes did business. I was so excited I couldn't even speak. I couldn't believe that it was finally for real.

We pulled into the warehouse parking lot and Dad drove around to the back. There, parked by itself, sat the most amazing Volkswagen Beetle I had ever seen. It was baby blue with a white roof and dark blue racing stripes on the side. The car was perfectly shaped in a smooth half oval. There wasn't a dent or ust spot on it.

"Is that it?" I squealed. "It's beautiful!"

Dad laughed.

"I knew you would like it. Did you think I would get anything less for my number one girl?"

Before he could bring the station wagon to a complete stop, I flung open the door and jumped out. I raced to the Volkswagen and peered into the driver's side window, taking in the black vinyl interior. Then I made a circle around the car, running my hands along the stripes and over the hood, which radiated warmth from the Texas sun.

"I love it, Dad!" I yelled, turning back to look at him. "This is so cool. I can't believe it's for real."

He beamed. "Well, I promised you I would get you a car. Now I just have to come up with the money to get the motor fixed."

My whole body tingled. I felt dizzy with happiness. I wanted to dance and sprint around the parking lot and whoop with joy. I had daydreamed about this day plenty of times, but my imagination never came close to matching the feelings I had inside. I ran to him and wrapped my arms around his waist.

"Thank you, thank you, thank you! I don't even know what to say. This means everything to me."

Dad squeezed me back. "Well, we're here. You might as well go get to know your car." He pulled out a key from his pocket and handed it to me.

The words "your car" replayed in my mind as I raced back to the VW. I opened the driver's side door, climbed in, and spent the next few minutes going over every detail. I moved the seat forward until I had it adjusted to my height. I played with the radio knob and moved the switch on the heater. I opened the glove compartment and put my wallet in it while I pretended to be driving.

"I want to show you something," Dad called from behind the car.

I climbed out and walked to where he was standing. He popped open the trunk and exposed the Beetle's secret—the fact that the engine was actually located in the back instead of the front like every other car I had seen.

"Here's where the oil goes," he said, unscrewing the lid to the motor oil compartment. Then he pulled out the oil stick so he could show me where to keep the oil level.

"If you don't remember anything else, remember to always keep the oil level up in your car and change it on a regular basis. I've seen more vehicles ruined by that than anything else."

"Okay, Dad," I said, only half listening as I headed to the front of the car to check out the storage compartment. The car was so perfect I considered pinching myself to make sure I hadn't reverted into one of my daydreams.

I glanced back at Dad, who was still standing by the engine. He looked as happy as I felt.

I could have spent the night in the car, or the rest of my summer camped out beside it—just to make sure that nothing happened to it. But after forty-five minutes, Dad told me it was time to go.

"Don't worry," he said as we drove out of the parking lot. "It's yours. And one way or another, I'll get it fixed. You'll be driving it soon enough."

Dad and I spent the next couple of weeks testing out his new business venture. We traveled our usual loops through Oklahoma and Kansas, but instead of searching for oil rigs, we popped into every small or mid-sized town we came across and kept our eyes peeled for mom-and-pop gas stations and independent truck stops.

As Dad predicted, it wasn't too hard to get the store owners to invest a few dollars in sunglasses and T-shirts, and soon money was flowing again.

Dad told me he had been thinking about Rhonda and feeling a little guilty for not being in touch for so long, so he decided to surprise her by wiring her three hundred dollars. A few days later, when Dad called to check in with Harold, he learned that Rhonda had sent divorce papers.

"I guess she used the money I wired her to file for the divorce," Dad said as he hung up the phone. "I'm a little surprised. But to tell you the truth, Ingrid, I'm also a little relieved. There wasn't anything there anyway, and now I don't have to worry about supporting her."

He laughed. "Yup, Ingrid. It's just the way it goes."

The next morning, he announced that we were heading to Amarillo so he could visit Debbie, the twenty-two-year-old AT&T operator who had tracked him down at the Iowa Holiday Inn five weeks earlier.

I pictured an aggressive, stalker-type woman, but Debbie was the last thing from that. She was quiet and came across as shy. Unlike Rhonda or the other women I had seen Dad with, Debbie wasn't into the glamorous look. She wore little, if any, makeup, and had short, brown hair that looked like it didn't require more than a few brush strokes to style. Her fingernails were short and she was dressed in a conservative blouse, jeans, and comfortable-looking flats. And she looked young. Really young. Then again, Dad had said she was only six years older than me.

"Hi," I said, extending my hand. "I'm Ingrid. Jerry's daughter."

"Hi there," she said softly. Her accent immediately reminded me of living in Mississippi.

"Debbie's from Tennessee," Dad said, guessing my question. "From a little town just outside Nashville."

It took only a few days in Amarillo with Debbie to convince Dad that he should make the west Texas town his base. That meant heading back to Fort Worth to restock on merchandise. It also meant trading in the station wagon for a truck so Dad could tow my Volkswagen to Amarillo and get it to a mechanic he knew there.

"Here's what I'm thinking," Dad said as we drove back to Amarillo two days later in the Dodge pickup he had just acquired, with my car safely hitched behind it. "I figure it will cost about three hundred dollars to fix your car and that it'll be ready in about a week. That will give me a few days to earn some extra cash. Then what I'll do is drive that old Chevy Vega I just picked up back to Utah to give to your sister, and you can follow behind me like you did when we drove to Iowa."

Dad was always acquiring junk vehicles. He liked to have them handy in case something happened to the one he was driving or someone he knew needed one. Just before leaving Amarillo to pick up my Volkswagen in Fort Worth, Dad had given a guy some tools in exchange for the Vega. I didn't realize then that the car was for Connie.

"Yup, that's what I'm thinking, Ingrid," he continued. "I know Connie's been needing another car real bad and when I talked to her last, I promised I'd get her one. And this way I can visit with your brothers and sisters for a few days and then fly back to Texas."

His words were like magic dust. I was so excited I could hardly think straight. Ever since he had told me about my car early in the summer, he'd promised that we would be driving it back to Utah. But it hadn't seemed real until now. And the idea of driving the eight hundred miles by myself, in my own car, following behind him sent a rush through me. Ever since driving the Pinto to Iowa, I had been fantasizing about the thrill of taking my own car out on a road trip.

We pulled into Amarillo around noon and dropped my car with the mechanic, who told Dad he would give it a good look that night and provide his assessment the next morning. That evening, while Dad was out on a date with Debbie, I lay in my motel room bed thinking about the excitement that awaited me. In only ten days, I would be starting my junior year of high school. And I was going to be starting it with my new car.

I loved that my car had the trunk in the front of it. And it was a big trunk that could hold plenty of gear if I decided to take off on a long road trip somewhere with Heather. I couldn't wait to show her. I was going to head to her house the minute I pulled into Logan and take her for a ride. I would probably even pick her up for the first day of school.

At eight the next morning, Dad and I drove over to the mechanic shop to get the scoop on my car. When the guy told Dad that the engine was completely shot and it was going to cost eight hundred and fifty dollars to fix, I thought his veins were going to pop out of his neck.

"What do you mean eight hundred and fifty dollars?" Dad nearly screamed at the mechanic. "How can it cost eight hundred and fifty dollars? I don't have that kind of money!"

I stood quietly beside Dad, feeling my heart sink. He didn't have to say anything as we walked back to the truck. The cost was nearly triple what he had expected to pay. I knew there was no way Dad could get his hands on that kind of money. Especially now. His court hearing was two months away and he had to figure out how to repay the ten grand he owed the bank or this time he really was going to jail.

He looked like the air had been knocked out of him.

"I can't believe he wants that much money to fix that car," he muttered under his breath.

My heart felt like it had dropped into my gut, but I concentrated on keeping my face neutral so Dad wouldn't see how disappointed I was. We drove in silence for a minute. I knew he was trying to find the right words to let me down, and I realized I should speak up first and tell him it was okay and I understood, but I couldn't make the words come out.

Dad finally spoke. "You know I want to get that car fixed for you as much as you do. But I just don't know how I'm going to be able to come up with that kind of money in a week. I'm sorry, Ingrid. But I'm going to have to bring it up to you in a couple of months."

I reached for his hand and squeezed it. As bad as I felt about the car, seeing his disappointment made me feel worse.

"It's okay, Dad," I said, trying to make my voice sound light and positive. "I know you can't do anything about it right now. And what's a couple of months anyway?"

I spent the next two days trying to ignore the ache in my gut. Along with the crushing disappointment over not being able to have my car for a while, I was depressed about being cheated out of driving it back to Utah. I'd been looking forward to the road trip and had prepped for it over and over in my mind. Then, with less than a week to go before school started, it hit me that there was still a way to salvage the trip home. While I wouldn't be able to drive my Volkswagen back to Utah, maybe there was a chance I could drive the Chevy Vega back to Utah for Connie.

I knew Dad still needed to get the car to her. I also knew that he was so squeezed financially that he'd decided he couldn't afford to take the time off from selling to drive with me to Utah. And he certainly didn't have money to fly himself back.

Dad had mentioned the possibility of sending me home by bus. But this still didn't address his need to get the Chevy to

Utah and I knew that was my trump card. I waited until his mood seemed right before approaching him.

"I have an idea," I said, trying to act as though the thought had just occurred to me. "Why don't I drive the Vega back to Utah? This way, you kill two birds with one stone. I get home in time for school and Connie has her car, so you don't have to worry about how you're going to get it to her."

Dad didn't say anything, but I could see his mind working.

"Please," I begged. "It's a perfect solution and you know I can do it. I mean, I drove that other car across two states by myself. And that was when I had just got my license."

"That's true, but I was right there with you in case anything went wrong," Dad said.

"Nothing's going to happen, Dad. How long have I been out here on the road with you? You know I can take care of myself."

Dad was quiet again, but I knew I had planted a seed. I also knew how hard it was for him to say "no." And the truth was, my plan did solve two problems for him.

Two more days passed and Dad still hadn't given me his answer. School was starting in four days, and Mom was furious that I was still in Texas and Dad didn't have a plan for getting me back to Utah. She had even called my uncle and asked him to loan Dad the money for a bus ticket for me.

That pissed off Dad.

"Well, if you're going to be driving that Chevy back to Utah, we better take it out for a practice run to make sure you feel comfortable," he announced the next morning.

I wanted to do a victory dance but I could tell by the serious look on Dad's face that exhibiting too much enthusiasm would be a bad idea. I concentrated on keeping my voice steady and firm.

"I think it's a good plan, Dad."

"I just hope I won't regret it," he mumbled.

"You won't, Dad, I promise."

We drove to a car lot where the Chevy Vega was parked so I could get a feel for it. I hopped in and discovered that I couldn't reach the pedals. When I tried to shift the seat forward, I realized it was broken.

"It's okay, I can just stick my duffel bag behind me," I said quickly, not wanting to give Dad any reason to change his mind.

Dad showed me the trick to starting the car. I first had to insert the key into the ignition and turn it to the "on" position. Then I had to push the red button hidden in the glove box which was connected to two wires. Dad warned me not to mess with the wires because he said if they got disconnected, the car wasn't going anywhere. The next minor issue was the stick shift. The knob at the top of the stick was broken and popped off in my hand during my first practice ride around the parking lot. I made a mental note to always push down on the knob when shifting so it didn't come off on me when I was driving down the freeway. I finished my test drive and arrived back to where Dad was waiting for me.

"What do you think?"

"I think it's perfect, Dad. It drives fine and everything's great. It's not going to be a problem at all."

"Well, I know one thing that's not fine," Dad said. "I'm going to have to fix that radio so that you have some music to keep you company. Otherwise, it's going to be a long drive."

Dad spent the next hour hooking up loose wires on the radio until we got reception. Then I followed Dad to a nearby gas station so he could fill up the tank and check the air in the tires to make sure they were good to go. Afterward, we headed back to our motel room so I could pack and get ready for my adventure.

That night, Dad gave me a road atlas and had me show him the route I would be taking so he felt comfortable that I knew where I was going. Then he handed me two crisp, fifty dollar bills.

"Here's some money to get you home. It should be plenty to cover you for gas, food, and a motel room for a night. Whatever you don't spend, you can keep."

I fingered the bills in my hands. They felt brand-new, like they had been issued just for this trip.

"Thanks, Dad." I pulled out my wallet from my denim purse and carefully tucked the money into the billfold behind my driver's license.

"Whatever you do, don't lose that money," Dad's voice trailed behind me. In my mind, I was already gone.

I set my alarm clock for 3:30 A.M., but I was so excited I woke up before it went off. I quickly showered, threw on a pair of shorts and a T-shirt, and then woke up Dad. By 4 A.M., I was by the door with my duffel bag.

"So you ready to put some miles behind you?" Dad asked as he walked me to the car.

"Oh, I'm ready," I said with a grin on my face. "This is going to be the best day of my life."

"I hope you're right," he replied, giving me a hug.

I opened the car door, arranged my duffel bag behind me, and got in. I reached the pedals perfectly. I started the car and then waited for Dad to pull out so I could follow him to the freeway. Dad wanted to make sure that I at least got off in the right direction.

When we arrived at the on-ramp, he pulled off to the side of the road and I followed his lead. I watched him get out of the car and make his way to my car window. He looked concerned and tense.

"Are you sure you are going to be all right, Ingrid?"

"Yes, Dad. I promise," I said, trying not to sound exasperated. "You don't need to worry about me. Everything is going to be great."

"Okay," he said and sighed, sounding a lot less confident than he had been when we left the motel. "Here's what I want you to do," he said, suddenly sounding stern and serious. "The minute you get even a little bit tired or sleepy, I want you to pull off to a rest area or go somewhere and relax. If you need to, just stop and get a motel room. And I want you to call and check in with me at 4 p.m. sharp. I'll be at Debbie's house. You can call me there." He handed me a piece of paper with Debbie's phone number scribbled on it.

"Okay, sounds great, Dad. I will."

I was getting antsy and wanted to start my drive. I worried that the longer we waited around, the more likely it was that Dad would change his mind. I reached through my rolled down window and gave Dad another hug.

"I love you, Dad. And thanks again for letting me do this. This is the best adventure I could wish for."

"Okay, Ingrid. I love you, too."

Dad finally walked back to his car. The minute he closed the car door behind him, I was gone.

"YES!" I shouted into the quiet darkness. "I'm doing it!"

A jolt of energy rushed through me. I had never felt so free. Or so happy. I was where I belonged.

For a while, I lost myself in the white and yellow lines that stretched endlessly on the concrete in front of me. I loved those lines. They were like old friends beckoning me to keep on coming toward them. Those lines had kept Dad and me going for years. Along with the mystery of the unknown that awaited us, they held the hope for a better future—one where Dad finally achieved his million-dollar dream and I was free of Earl and the poverty at home.

My mind jumped to Mom and how surprised she was going to be when she saw me pull up to the house in the car. She knew I was on my way home, and Connie knew she was getting her car, but they both just assumed Dad had finally decided to bring me. They had no idea I was coming on my own.

My thoughts drifted to the journey ahead of me. I had a little more than nine hundred miles to drive. I figured I could cover at least six hundred miles today and then drive the rest of the way in the morning, arriving home just about the time everyone was returning from church. I couldn't wait to see the look on their faces.

I leaned back against my duffel bag, which I had arranged vertically so it covered the length of the seat. Every cell in my body felt alive. I listened to the sound of the early morning silence, interrupted only by the roar of the occasional semitruck that passed by me.

I loved this time of day. The air smelled clean and fresh and was still cool on my skin, but I knew that once the sun came up, it was going to get hot, and I wanted to savor the moments.

I pushed my foot down on the gas pedal to see how fast I could get the car to go. It had a good motor and drove smoothly even at seventy-five miles an hour. The speed limit was fifty-five and I made a mental note to keep a lookout for cops. I slowed down a little and waited a few minutes for a semitruck to pass me. Then I pulled in behind it and followed its lead. I knew this was my best protection against a speeding ticket because truck drivers always had their two-way radios going and alerted each other when a patrolman was spotted. I smiled, proud of my road knowledge. I felt savvy and smart and free.

A couple of hours into the drive, I decided it was time for music. I turned on the radio and scanned through a dozen country stations before landing on an oldies station that was playing, "I Want to Hold Your Hand." I belted out the Beatles tune as loud as I could. I had been a Beatles fan ever since I was six, when a hitchhiker Dad brought home to stay with us pulled out his guitar and sang "Michelle" to me because I had told him that Michelle was my middle name. At the time, I thought he had made up the song for me.

I rolled down my window and shouted the words into the morning air. I'm sure I was a sight, flying down the freeway in a beat-up pumpkin-orange car, my duffel bag shoved behind me for support, the seat so low that my head was barely visible over the steering wheel, my left arm hanging out the window to ride the waves the air made as I sped down the road. I didn't care. I was free and I could do anything I wanted and I was going to make the most of it.

I thought about my summer with Dad, which I had come to view in two distinct parts: Before His Arrest and After His Arrest. It felt like two separate worlds. Before his arrest, our summer had been just like any other summer we'd had together. Dad was my savior and my mentor and the person I depended on for my emotional survival. But on the day of his arrest—in the span of twelve hours—everything had changed.

I felt different now. I loved Dad as much as I had ever loved him, but there was a distance between us and I no longer counted on him to save me. I knew he felt the difference, too. The last part of the summer he had been pulling away from me and moving toward Debbie. I didn't mind. In fact I was glad that he had found someone else to spend time with.

I felt so much older now. I also felt strong and ready to get on with my life. For the first time in all the summers I had spent with Dad, I looked forward to getting home.

I thought about Heather and wondered what she had been doing while I was away. I couldn't wait to see her and start my junior year of high school. A couple of weeks earlier, I had received a letter from Heather that Mom had forwarded to me. Heather had told me that there was an open spot in Crimson Colony, a singing group at our high school that I was desperate to get into. Maybe I had a chance.

School was starting in two days. I couldn't believe it. Mom

had registered me for classes because I wasn't home, but we had discussed what I wanted to take over the phone.

The only bad part about going home was that Earl was still there. I hated it that after four years, he was still living in our house. Still unemployed. Still leeching off Mom. Still making life miserable for everyone around him. But I didn't feel the same anxiety that always took hold of me when I returned home after a summer with Dad. Instead of the usual stomach cramps and throbbing headache, I felt clear, calm, and relaxed.

I wasn't going to let Earl ruin my mood. He didn't scare me anymore. After a few hours on the road, I pulled off the freeway and headed to a 7-Eleven to fill up on gas and pick up a Sugar Free Dr Pepper and some chips. I spent a couple of minutes circling the parking lot, stretching my legs. Then I was off again.

I picked out another semitruck to follow and pushed the car back up to seventy-five miles an hour. I was making great time and started thinking about the possibility of making it all the way home in one day.

So far, I had spent only nineteen dollars and I figured if I could skip out on a motel room, it would give me at least fifty dollars I could pocket. Besides, I could just imagine how surprised Dad would be when I told him I'd made it home in a single day.

When I hit Albuquerque, I pulled into the first truck stop I came across and dug out the atlas Dad had given me. I used my fingers to chart my path through the bottom quarter of Colorado into Utah.

I headed into the truck stop for a drink and bathroom break, and spent a few minutes in the truck stop trading post, admiring the rows of moccasins. I considered splurging and buying myself a pair, but they were thirty dollars and I knew I would be pushing it moneywise. I pulled away from the moccasins and glanced around at the truckers—paying for fuel, talking on the pay phones, loading up on snacks. I might not have looked like them, but I felt like one of them. I understood why they lived their lives on the road. They were free.

I lingered for another fifteen minutes, watching the truckers come and go, and then decided to be on my way.

When I got back on the road again, I was in the mood for music and turned the radio knob. Nothing happened. The radio was dead. Dad's wiring job must have given out. I didn't care. I began humming whatever tune popped into my head.

After a while, my thoughts drifted to school. Homecoming was only a few weeks away and I wondered if I would get asked to go to the dance. I hoped so. It was the one dance that everyone wanted to go to, and if you didn't get asked, it looked bad.

I pushed the car through Southern Colorado, enjoying the changing landscape around me. It had gone from flat and dusty in West Texas to hilly with beautiful red rocks that erupted from the ground. That's what I loved about being out on the road. If you weren't partial to your surroundings, you could just keep on going until you found a spot you liked. You didn't have to stay in a place that made you unhappy.

I glanced at my watch. It was already 3 P.M. I couldn't believe how fast the day was flying. I was nearing the Utah border and calculated that if I kept going, I could make it home by midnight.

I reminded myself that Dad had told me to check in with him at 4 P.M., but I was making such good time that I didn't want to stop. I felt so free and energized and peaceful behind the wheel. I just wanted to keep driving.

I decided to surprise him with a call in a few hours, when I was closer to Logan. I knew he would be impressed when I told him how far I had made it.

The air was hot and at about 5 P.M., I began to get sleepy. I remembered Dad's words and pulled over to a gas station. But instead of closing my eyes for a few minutes, I purchased a forty-four-ounce fountain drink of Sugar Free Dr Pepper and loaded it with ice. Then I pulled out a few ice cubes and stuck them down the back of my shirt the way Mom had so she could keep awake when she'd driven us out to Mississippi.

That refreshed me and I continued on with my drive. I was set on making it all the way home, but by the time I pulled into Price, Utah, it was nearly 8 P.M., and I was so wiped out that I decided maybe a motel room wasn't such a bad idea. I was only four hours from Logan and could always get up early and make it there by mid-morning.

I drove through the streets of the old coal-mining town looking for the cheapest motel I could find. When I saw a sign advertising rooms for nineteen dollars and ninety-nine cents, I stopped. An old man was running the check-in desk. He seemed surprised when I asked him for a room and eyed me suspiciously, but he didn't say anything. He just pushed some paperwork toward me, asked to see my driver's license, took my money, and then handed me a key. I headed across the parking lot to my room. As soon as I was inside, I looked for a phone to call Dad. I realized there wasn't one and headed back to the office.

"I need to call my dad," I told the man. "Do you have a phone I can use?"

He looked me over again. "Is it long distance?"

"Yeah. But I can call collect."

He reached under the counter and pulled out a black rotary phone. Then he stood and watched as I carefully dialed the numbers scribbled on the piece of paper Dad had given me that morning. I preferred a little privacy and looked at the man, hoping he would get the hint and move away but he just stared at me.

The operator connected me and the phone answered on the first ring. I heard Dad answer a quick, "Yes" when she asked if he would accept the call.

"Ingrid?" Dad's voice sounded tense.

"Hi, Dad? How's it going? Guess where I'm at?"

"Why the hell didn't you call me at 4 P.M. like I told you to?" he thundered into the phone. "Do you realize that I've been worried sick all day about you? Your grandmother and mom are beside themselves they're so upset. I think they're about ready to crucify me. I should have never let you do this. What the hell were you thinking, Ingrid?"

My joy was sapped in an instant. I felt my hands trembling and fought back the lump that was making its way into my throat.

"Sorry, Dad," I mumbled into the phone. "I was just trying to surprise you. I thought I'd see if I could make it all the way to Logan."

"I'll say you surprised me!" he barked into the phone. "You

almost gave me a heart attack, that's how surprised I am. When I said to call at 4 P.M., I meant 4 P.M. Can you just try to imagine how worried we've all been? We thought something horrible had happened to you!

"Do you know that ten minutes after you left, I realized I had made the worst mistake of my life? I started coming after you but I got a flat on the freeway. I called your grandma and she chewed me out and then called your mom, who completely freaked out on me. Everybody's so angry and worried sick, you can't believe it."

My head was pounding and my body felt like lead. The adrenaline that had kept me going strong for the last sixteen hours was gone.

I glanced over at the old man, who tried to look busy scribbling something in his logbook. I knew he could hear Dad's tirade.

"You can't make it to Logan in one day!" he continued. "What in the hell were you thinking? And just how fast were you going anyway? Eighty miles an hour the whole way?"

I felt sick to my stomach. The last thing I'd expected was for Dad to be angry with me. I could see his point about not calling and I realized I should have done it. But I didn't mean to upset him and I couldn't believe he was so worked up. He knew I could take care of myself. It's not like I hadn't been in worse situations.

The mention of Mom really threw me off guard. All I needed was for her to be pissed off at me too. Plus, it completely blew my surprise plan. I had thought about timing my arrival so I would get home after church started. I was going to pull up to the house, stick on a dress, and head over to church in time for

Sacrament meeting. I had been picturing the happy surprise on her face.

"Where are you at right now?" Dad demanded, his voice still full of fire.

"At a motel in Price," I mumbled.

"Okay. I want you to get a room right this minute and I want you to promise me you will spend the night there. And in the morning, I want you to call me before you get on the road. Call me at 8 A.M. your time. And don't try to pull any other surprises either, because I'll know whether you are calling from the motel or somewhere else in the morning."

"Okay," I said and then hung up the phone.

I dragged myself back across the parking lot, unlocked the door to my room, walked in, shut the door, attached the dead bolt, and flung myself onto the double bed. I was so deflated and tired I didn't even have the energy to take off my clothes.

I awoke to pounding on my door. I looked through the peep-hole and saw the old man from the night before.

"Your dad is on the phone," he yelled.

I glanced at the clock. It was 8:05 A.M.

"Okay, thanks. I'll be right there," I returned.

I quickly splashed water on my face to wake myself up, sprinted across the parking lot to the reception office, and picked up the receiver.

"Hi, Dad. Sorry, I just got up."

"I thought you had tried to pull another surprise on me," he said, his voice considerably calmer than the night before. "Good thing you didn't, that's all I can say."

I hung up the phone, headed back to my room, and took a

long shower. At this point, I had no reason to hurry, so I took my time dressing and even spent an hour flipping through the TV channels.

After a couple of hours, I checked out, filled up on gas, swung by a McDonald's for an orange juice and sausage McMuffin, and then hit the road.

Since everyone was upset anyway, I decided I was going to savor the rest of my drive and I took my time getting to Logan. It was midafternoon when I pulled up to the house. Mom and Connie both came running out to meet me.

Connie had an impressed look on her face. Mom looked like she was ready to skin me alive.

"That was a stupid thing to do!" Mom spewed as soon as she got close to me. "You could have been killed. What were you thinking? Your dad should have known better than to let you go off like that."

"Hi, Mom," I said, offering her a halfhearted hug.

I turned to Connie, who was visiting for a few days before heading back to school in Southern Utah. She was already checking out her car.

"It drives great but you've got to push the red button in the glove box to start it," I told her, tossing her the key. "And you're going to have to do something about the seat and the radio because they're both broken."

I grabbed my duffel bag from the car and then headed to my room, leaving Mom and Connie standing outside. Nobody got it. I had just wrapped up the best day and a half of my life.

I called Heather to tell her I was back in town and make plans for the next day. Then I unpacked and started combing through my closet for an outfit to wear for the first day of school.

I didn't see Earl until dinner. We were sitting only three chairs apart, but neither of us acknowledged each other's presence.

Mom didn't say any more about my solo trip home and I didn't bring it up either. But when Dad called around eight that evening to check in, his mood had done a one-eighty.

"So are you still alive after your mom got through chewing you out?" he said, chuckling into the phone. "I'll tell you something, Ingrid. I'm glad I'm still alive. That was as close to a heart attack as I've ever had."

I smiled, glad that he was back to being in a good mood.

"I know I should have called you, Dad. I didn't mean to worry you. I just figured you would know I was fine."

"I wasn't worried about you," Dad huffed into the phone. "I know you can take care of yourself. I was worried about the piece-of-shit car you were driving. That pile of junk could have broken down when you were out in the middle of nowhere and then what would you have done?

"Yeah, I don't know how I let you talk me into that," he continued. "I don't think I'll ever live that down with your mom or grandma. But since everything turned out fine, I guess I made the right decision. And I definitely know it's one adventure you won't ever forget."

17

. . .

Soaking in our iron claw-foot tub had become a nightly ritual for me.

With only one bathroom and six people, getting more than five minutes alone in there each morning was unthinkable. But by 9 P.M., everyone was in bed and I had the room to myself.

I submerged my head into the steaming water until only my eyes, nose, and mouth were uncovered, and settled into my thoughts. In the two weeks I had been home, life had gone smoothly—maybe because I had finally figured out what Connie had discovered when she was in high school: There was a way to live in our house without really living there.

The secret was packing your day so full that you wouldn't have time to be at home. Since starting school, I had managed to skip most of our morning scripture sessions by telling Mom I had to be at school for an early morning study hour. After school, I either hung out with Heather or headed to the music room to practice for the upcoming music group tryouts. In the evenings, I could usually come up with some school game or booster club activity that I was supposed to participate in. And I had spent the two Saturdays I had been home walking through the mall with Heather collecting applications for a job. Along with earning spending money, I knew I needed steady income to cover my car insurance and gas once Dad brought up the Beetle.

I handled Earl like I did the year before: I pretended he didn't exist. Except my new strategy was even better because I was barely home, so I hardly ever had to see him. Aside from the occasional morning scripture session I still attended, the only time I encountered Earl now was at dinner. But he usually stuffed down his frog legs and deer meat without badgering us—maybe because Mom had finally had enough.

Mom barely spoke to him when I was around and it was impossible not to feel the tension between them. In addition to his "man rules" antics, I knew she had had all she could take of him tinkering on cars while she was pounding away forty to fifty hours a week trying to cover our expenses. We didn't talk about her money stresses, but she was back to her old habit of sitting at the kitchen table at night with the bills spread across it, studying them and looking for something to skip.

Thinking about Mom made me sad so I switched my thoughts to school. I loved being back in high school and it was great not to be a sophomore anymore. Classes were going well and Heather and I spent every free moment we had together. And we both had been asked to Homecoming.

I started thinking about my car, replaying images of it in my mind. I worried about it sitting at the mechanic shop in Amarillo. What if someone stole it before Dad had the money to fix it? The last time Dad had called, he said he was still working on raising the eight hundred and fifty dollars to fix the engine.

"Believe me, I want you to have your car as bad as you do," he had said into the phone, sensing my disappointment. "It's just that business is a little slow right now. But I'm thinking I should be able to have it ready to bring up to you the first week in October. In fact, let's just plan on that, okay?"

As I submerged myself in the old tub, water enveloped my body like a cocoon and I didn't want to move. But the temperature had gone from steaming to lukewarm and my efforts to turn on the hot water faucet with my toes weren't working. I reluctantly pulled my head out of the water and sat up.

The cold air that greeted me carried with it angry whispers from Mom's bedroom. Our bathroom was sandwiched between her room and the kitchen, with doors leading to both, and the walls were so poorly insulated that it was usually impossible to block out the noise from the adjoining rooms. But Mom and Earl's heated whispers jumbled their voices, making it difficult to decipher their words.

I forgot about needing hot water and strained my ears, hoping to catch the gist of their argument. About five minutes into their hissing match, I heard Earl say my name, though I couldn't make out what he said next. "Just leave her alone!" I heard Mom respond in a raised, angry voice. Then I heard the sound that shot through my body like a bullet. It was the sound of a hand

Ingrid Ricks

slapping flesh. The last noise I heard was a small yelp from Mom. Then I was out of my body, watching myself transform into the same Incredible Hulk character I had seen Dad morph into so many times when I was younger.

I heard myself screaming as I leaped out of the tub, threw on my robe, and almost busted the lock on the door leading to the kitchen in my desperation to escape the room.

"Everybody is going to know what's going on in this house!" I screamed as I flew to the sewing room closet where the phone was hidden.

I grabbed the phone and the church directory, set them down on the kitchen table, and frantically began flipping through the pages looking for Bishop Whitten's home phone number. I didn't care that I was getting him out of bed. Someone had to stop this.

"PUT DOWN THAT PHONE!" Earl screamed, rushing toward me. I concentrated on the phone receiver, desperately punching in numbers.

I felt the receiver ripped from my hand and watched as the phone cord was yanked from the wall. The phone crashed to the ground just as Earl's fist connected with my stomach.

His punch was like fuel, stoking the hate burning through my body. I felt my fingers curl into tight fists and swing back at him, four years of rage packed inside them.

"GET OUT OF THIS HOUSE!" I yelled as my fists flew toward him. "GET OUT!"

Time slowed. I felt his fists smack against my shoulders and an occasional sharp pain when one landed on my ribs. But I also felt the sting from my fists hitting him. And it felt good.

Our plastic banquet table and chairs shot across the room as we crashed into them. Sometimes I felt my body hit the kitchen wall as we collided into each other and anything in our way.

I didn't know how much time had lapsed. I didn't think about where Mom had disappeared to, but the hits coming from Earl started to subside. I was exhausted and welcomed the break. Earl turned his attention to the bathroom door. I hadn't realized that Mom had locked herself in the bathroom until he began pounding on the door like it was his new punching bag.

"I want you to come out of there right now!" he ordered. "Right now! Do you hear me?"

I stared at the door, envisioning Mom kneeling by the bathtub praying. First I heard nothing coming from the bathroom. Then, after a few minutes that felt like hours, I heard the doorknob turn and watched Mom step out.

Her eyes were swollen but she was no longer crying. She looked strong. She turned to face Earl and I recognized the same burning hatred in her eyes.

"I want you to leave. Now."

She didn't raise her voice but her words were powerful and firm. We both stared at Earl, silently daring him to defy her.

He started to protest and then stopped. After a long minute, he turned and walked out of the house.

The second the front door slammed shut, Heidi and Jacob came running into the kitchen.

"What's going on? What happened?" Heidi asked, looking from Mom to me.

"Is everything okay?"

Mom didn't speak. She looked like she was in some sort of a trance. "Everything's fine," I answered. "He's gone."

"I'm going to bed," I added, suddenly drained. I turned and made a beeline for my attic room.

I was a little sore and bruised when I woke up the next morning, but I felt light, as though I had just been freed from a crushing weight.

I decided to skip my early morning at school and attend scripture reading, figuring that Mom would want to talk about what had happened and discuss her plans for divorcing Earl. But she didn't say a word about it. She just passed out the hymnbooks and *The Book of Mormon*.

"Who wants to pick the opening song?" she asked, ignoring the quizzical looks both Heidi and I were shooting her.

I started to say something, but stopped myself. It was clearly an emotional time for Mom and I didn't want to remind her of the nightmare we had all just been through. Just knowing that Earl was finally gone was good enough for me.

Two days later, I walked into the house after spending the afternoon with Heather and found Earl standing in the kitchen next to Mom.

Seeing him stopped me in my tracks. I felt my body start to tremble and my fingernails dig into the palms of my hands.

I looked at Mom in disbelief. Our eyes locked for a second and then she looked away.

Fire shot through my body. I felt the monster overtaking me again.

"If he's stays, I go!" I stammered, my voice half threatening, half pleading.

Mom didn't respond. Earl just stared at me with his icy-blue eyes and smiled.

I stormed out of the kitchen and spent the evening holed up in my room, alternating between panic and rage. My brain felt heavy and I couldn't concentrate. I just needed to calm down and think rationally so I could figure out what to do.

I couldn't believe this was happening. How could Mom let him come back? What was wrong with her?

Where was I going to go? What was Heidi going to do? What about Jacob and Daniel? How could any of us live here any longer?

My mind wouldn't focus. My head hurt and I was too exhausted to formulate a plan. I sat in my familiar spot with my back up against my bedroom door to prevent anyone from barging in.

Think. I just had to think.

That's when I remembered that the next day was Saturday. Heather and I had both been invited to a birthday slumber party and her dad had offered to give us a ride there. He was picking me up early, around noon, so we could shop for a present first.

That would give me most of the weekend to figure out what to do. Satisfied that I had made some progress, I climbed into bed and let myself fall sleep.

Mom didn't summon me to scripture reading the next morning and I wouldn't have gone anyway. I woke up late, hurried downstairs to grab a bowl of cereal, and then headed back to my room to eat and pack for my overnight escape.

My immediate shock and rage had subsided and I started thinking through my options. I now had my driver's license, which meant that maybe I could live with Grandma and still go to my high school. But I was without a car, even though I expected it in a couple of weeks. But my moving in with Grandma wouldn't help Heidi or my brothers.

I stayed in my room until I saw Heather's car pull up in front of the house. I sprinted down the stairs and out the door without saying a word to Mom.

"How's it going?" Heather asked as I climbed into the backseat.

"Great," I answered, trying to make my voice sound light. I wasn't about to get into my problems with her dad there. Plus we'd been looking forward to the party all week and I didn't want to be a downer.

I decided to push my dilemma to the back of my mind and just have some fun for a change. I spent the rest of the day playing games, eating pizza, watching movies, and laughing with friends. We didn't go to sleep until after 2 A.M. and by the time we woke up, it was past noon—well past church time.

I still didn't have a plan but I was toying with asking Heather if I could hang out at her place for a couple days. I was so upset at Mom for letting Earl back into the house that I wasn't sure I was ready to speak to her. But I was also worried about her and I was feeling a little guilty for leaving the house without saying anything.

I decided to give her a call—just to let her know I was okay—and asked to use my friend's phone. I felt my fingers shaking as I slowed dialed the number. I hoped Earl wouldn't answer the phone. If he did, I knew I would slam the receiver down.

The phone rang four times before it was answered. "Hello?"

It was Connie's voice.

"What are you doing there?" I asked, relief washing over me. I knew she was in town visiting friends for the weekend, but I didn't expect her to be at the house.

"I saw Mom last night and figured I'd hang around here and help her out a little," Connie replied coyly.

I wasn't sure what she was getting at. "What do you mean? Is everything okay?"

"I would say great," Connie almost sang into the phone. "Mom's getting a divorce."

Her words were so unexpected I almost didn't know how to respond. "Are you serious? Please say you're serious."

I pressed the receiver hard against my ear to make certain I was hearing her right.

"Completely serious," she replied. "Mom's already told him."

"So what happened?" I asked, still unable to fully grasp what she was telling me. "Why the sudden switch?"

"Well, I stopped by the house for a visit yesterday afternoon and the minute I looked at Mom, I could tell she was miserable. So I invited her to take a little drive with me so she could get away from Earl and talk.

"As soon as we were a block from the house, I asked her why she didn't just get a divorce," Connie continued. "She said she couldn't because of her temple marriage. She said she couldn't just go to the bishop and tell him she had made another mistake and wanted to divorce this husband too."

"Yeah, that figures," I replied, seething at the thought. "So what did you say to her?"

"I didn't say anything to her, but it got me thinking. I realized that the only way a divorce would happen is if the bishop told her it was okay, so this morning before church, I paid him a little visit and explained what was going on. When I was done talking, Bishop Whitten told me he knew the situation with Earl was a bad one and said he would have never allowed the temple marriage to take place had he been the bishop at the time. But he added that he didn't have the right to advise Mom to divorce Earl unless she came to him asking for help."

"So what did you do? How did you get Mom to ask him for help?"

Connie laughed. "Well, it was clear that neither one of them was going to make the first move, so I decided to do it for them. Before leaving the bishop's office, I told him to expect Mom in his office as soon as Sacrament meeting was over. Then I went to Mom, told her that the bishop was unhappy with her marriage to Earl, and said that he wanted to talk with her as soon as church ended."

Connie's story floored me. I couldn't believe she had orchestrated the whole thing. I wanted to climb through the phone line and high-five her—maybe award her with a Sister of the Year ribbon or something.

I listened intently as Connie continued her story. "Mom was nervous about going to the bishop's office, so she waited in the hall outside his office door. Finally he came out and asked her if she wanted to see him and she nodded her head. That was all it took. When she came out a few minutes later, she told me she was getting a divorce. And with the bishop backing her, there's no way Earl dares to defy her."

I said good-bye to Connie, hung up the phone, and sat in silence, letting the news soak in. The relief that washed over me was so powerful that it muted any other emotion I had inside.

Because of Connie, it was over. I didn't have to find a new place to live. By the time I arrived home late that afternoon, Earl was gone. So was Connie. She had left an hour earlier to head back to school.

As soon as I walked into the house, Mom called my brothers, Heidi, and me into the living room to talk.

She looked relieved but serious.

"Earl and I are separating," she said quietly, looking at the ground as she spoke. "He's already taken his belongings out of the house and he's going to come by tomorrow while I'm at work to get his tools from the garage."

I wanted to celebrate, to do a victory dance—something to mark the occasion. But I could tell Mom wasn't in a celebrating mood.

"Thank you, Mom," I said quietly, moving beside her to give her a hug. "I know things are going to get better now."

The tension and depression that had clogged the air in our house were gone as soon as Earl moved out.

The most noticeable change was with Mom. It was like the chains had been removed. For the first time in nearly four years, she moved through the house like she owned it instead of like someone being held in captivity there. Everything from the way she carried herself to the way she interacted with us was different. I recognized the new expression she wore on her face: hope.

That Saturday, Mom drove me to Winchell's, a local donut shop, so I could apply for a job. A few days later, I received a call from the manager offering me the Saturday/Sunday weekend shift. The old mom would have forbidden me to take the job because it meant working on Sunday. But this new, hopeful Mom congratulated me and even offered to give me a ride to and from work.

"Thanks, Mom," I said, hugging her. "I really appreciate it. I'll only need a ride for a week or two—just until Dad brings me my car."

She didn't say anything but I could tell she didn't believe me.

Dad came to visit the first week in October like he said he would. Debbie was with him. My car wasn't.

"I'm still working on getting your car fixed, Ingrid," Dad explained when he saw the devastated look on my face. "You know I've got that hearing coming up at the end of this month and right now figuring out how to pay that back is more important. Don't worry, though. You'll get that car. It's a promise."

I tried to ignore the ache in my gut, but it was hard. I could see my car in my mind. I had memorized every detail of it during the hour I'd spent with it in that Fort Worth parking lot. Sometimes I would close my eyes and imagine my hands running along the dark blue racing stripes. I would envision my head resting against the black vinyl headrest and could hear in my mind the music playing from the radio.

Whenever I felt doubt creeping up inside me, I quickly shut it out. Dad had promised me that car and he had to come through. He just had to.

Like he had always done, Dad continued to call home once a week to check in and say hello. I always enjoyed hearing his voice, but it was impossible not to notice the change in our relationship. It had started with his arrest, but it was especially apparent now that Earl was gone. Without the misery at home, I no longer needed to escape my life. I knew Dad no longer needed me in the same way either. He had Debbie now.

In late October, Dad called to tell me his good news: He had worked things out with the court over the bank charge. He told me that he had explained to the judge during his hearing that it was his ex-employee, not him, who had pulled off the check-kiting scheme. But he said he also made it clear that he wanted to make things right with the bank. In the end, the judge waived jail time and agreed to let Dad repay the ten thousand dollar debt in installments of three hundred dollars a month.

When Dad called the next week, he said he had more good news: He and Debbie were married.

"Yup, Ingrid, we just decided to go for it," he said into the phone. "You know, when you get to be my age and you find someone you are compatible with, sometimes it's pretty clear what the right thing to do is. And Debbie's certainly the right partner for me, I can tell you that much. In a lot of ways, she reminds me of you, Ingrid. She wants to support me in anything I do."

As I let his words settle in, I realized the only emotion I felt was relief. Neither of us had mentioned it, but we both knew our summers together were over. I was glad he had found someone to keep him company and take care of him.

"So is she going to join up with you on the road? Or are you planning on just continuing to work around Amarillo for a while?"

"Oh, there's no business in Amarillo, Ingrid. The mom-and-pop shops around there have their own suppliers and don't want anything to do with the merchandise I'm selling. But that's part of what makes Debbie so great. She just took a six-month leave from work so she could travel and work with me. Isn't that something?"

"Yeah, that's great, Dad. Really great," I said, meaning every word. "She sounds like the perfect match for you."

18

. . .

I awoke with a smile on my face. It was Saturday, but for once I had the day off from work and I planned to kick back and relax for a while and then spend my afternoon with Heather—maybe head to the mall to do some shopping and catch a movie.

I peeked out the dormer window of my attic bedroom and saw that it had snowed the night before, blanketing the ground with a fresh coat of white powder. Then I noticed something else: a baby-blue Super Beetle with navy racing stripes parked in front of the house, partially covered in snow.

It took a moment for the shock to subside. Dad had told me he was coming up for Thanksgiving, but that was still five days away. I knew it was my car, though. I would have known that car anywhere.

I threw on my bathrobe and skipped down the wooden steps. "Mom! It's my car! Dad brought it! It's out in front!"

"What are you talking about?" Mom asked, poking her head out from her bedroom door.

"It's my Volkswagen! It's in front of the house!"

Before she could respond, I was on the phone, dialing the number to Grandma's house. Dad had to be in town, and if he was, that's where I expected to find him.

He answered the phone on the first ring, as though he had been waiting for my call.

"So did you find a surprise waiting for you this morning?" he said with a chuckle.

"I can't even believe it, Dad!" I gushed into the phone. "I can't believe it's real. I just can't believe it!"

Dad's voice went quiet for a minute.

"You didn't lose faith in me, did you?"

"No, of course not," I replied quickly. "It's just that it's been such a long time and I know that you've been under a lot of stress and I know it cost a lot of money to fix."

"Well, I promised it to you, didn't I?" Dad said softly. "I knew you wouldn't want to wait to take it out for a drive so I left the key in the glove compartment," he continued. "It drives fine but there's something wrong with the power so you're probably going to have to get that checked out."

"Thanks, Dad," I said again, so excited I could barely contain myself. "Thank you so much. You have no idea what this means to me."

I could feel his smile through the phone line.

"I'm glad I could do this for you, Ingrid. But the person you really ought to thank is Debbie. She's the one who gave me the money to get it fixed for you."

I felt a twinge of guilt when he said that. I didn't want it to be Debbie who paid for my car. This was Dad's gift to me—the exchange for the child support he hadn't been able to pay. The gift that he promised would set me free.

"Okay, tell her thank you for me," I said into the phone. "That was really nice of her to give you the money to get it fixed. And thanks again, Dad. I know how hard it was for you to make this happen."

We were both silent for a minute, maybe because we both recognized what the car symbolized: We had reached a fork in the road and it was time to part ways.

"So what are you still doing talking to me?" Dad said, breaking the awkwardness that had blanketed the phone line. "I thought you'd already be out there taking your car for a test drive."

"Okay, okay, I'm going," I said with a laugh.

I hung up the receiver, sprinted down the hall, and grabbed a pair of winter boots sitting in the laundry basket Mom kept by the front door.

I shoved my feet into them, swung open the door, and ran through the snow to my car.

"Finally," I whispered as I brushed the snow off the driver's side door handle with the sleeve of my robe.

After a few hard tugs on the frozen handle, I managed to pry the door open and quickly claimed my spot on the black vinyl driver's seat.

I opened the glove compartment just to make sure the key was really there. Then I leaned back into the headrest, took a deep breath, and kept my body still, letting my happiness seep through me, all the way into my fingers and toes.

I hadn't even put the key in the ignition yet. But I knew I had made it to my destination.

I closed my eyes and whispered a thank-you prayer to the universe.

EPILOGUE

· · ·

Summer 1984

The ferry ride to Victoria, British Columbia, was breathtaking. I stood on the deck with Heather, listening to the crashing waves as the fresh air rushed against my face—carrying with it the smell of saltwater that I would come to associate with a fresh start.

It was the summer before my senior year of high school, only a year since Dad's arrest and my final confrontation with Earl. But that seemed like a lifetime ago.

Though Dad still called home on a regular basis to check in, I hadn't seen much of him since he had surprised me with my car. Just before her six-month leave was up, Debbie had quit her job as a telephone operator and had taken my place as his sales partner. They now crisscrossed the highways of the Midwest together, spending most nights sleeping in the back of the van

Dad had recently swapped his truck for as they chased his million dollar dream.

Without Earl to drag down our days at home, the school year had flown by. I had worked twenty hours a week at the donut shop, and when not there or at school, I was with Heather—heading to the mall, going to the movies, hanging out, or cruising town in my beloved Volkswagen Beetle.

Mom still carried a heavy workload at the Health Department, but her smile was back and the dark circles were gone from under her eyes. She was still untangling herself from her marriage with Earl and was in no hurry to jump back into dating. After nearly four years of slavery, Mom—like the rest of us—was savoring her freedom.

Like the five summers before, I said good-bye to Mom shortly after school let out. But this time, I wasn't headed to the Midwest to sell tools with Dad. I was embarking on a three-week vacation—the first real vacation of my life.

Heather's family had invited me to accompany them on their annual summer trip to their cabin in Canada. More and more, she and her parents were like a family to me.

Heather's dad continued to correct my grammar whenever I misspoke and often talked about the importance of getting a college education. At home, we never discussed college. But Heather was in AP classes at school and it was a given that she would be going. And because of that, I knew I would be going too, and that one way or another, I was going to earn my college degree.

I felt the sun mixing with the wind and saltwater on my cheeks as I looked out at the beautiful scenery, taking in the rugged Olympic Mountains that framed the ocean inlet. I thought about how free and perfect life seemed, and how amazing it would be to live in the Pacific Northwest.

I thought about Connie, who had recently quit the community college she was attending and moved back to Jackson Hole, Wyoming. I understood now why she had decided to go back there. It made her feel what I was feeling now: free.

I remembered what she had told me about arriving in Jackson that first day after graduating from high school. She said she'd been walking into town with her friend Liz to grab some lunch and felt like she could finally breathe.

"It was like having all these burdens just go away all at once," she told me, struggling to put her feelings into words. "It was like this crushing weight I had lived with for so long was just suddenly gone. I felt so free. And so happy."

My thoughts turned to Heidi and my brothers. Heidi had just graduated from ninth grade and would be starting high school soon. She was still dealing with her asthma, but her asthma attacks were less frequent, and though we didn't talk much, she appeared happy. I knew she had a group of friends she hung around with now. Jacob was as quiet and serious as ever, but I noticed that his face seemed lighter. Daniel was still everyone's favorite. He would be turning seven soon and I was grateful that he would be celebrating his birthday without Earl in the house.

"You are going to love Victoria," Heather said, interrupting my thoughts. "It has the feel of a European city. And wait until we get to Butchart Gardens. They're the most amazing gardens you've ever seen."

The only garden I had experience with was the half-acre

vegetable garden Mom had planted in our backyard, and the idea of paying someone to see their garden was foreign to me. This trip had already been filled with a lot of firsts: My first visit to a Chinese restaurant. My first taste of seafood. My first ferry ride. My first trip to another country. A new world was opening up to me and I was determined to take it all in.

I thought about Dad and his obsession with becoming a successful, wealthy businessman. My gut ached for him sometimes. He worked so hard, harder than anyone I knew. I hoped it would happen for him. It had to happen for him.

Sometimes I missed being out on the open road, the rush of climbing into a car in the still-dark morning, hitting the gas pedal and just going—without knowing where I would end up. I didn't yet know what kind of career I wanted as an adult, but whatever it was, I knew I would have to be free. I couldn't sit in an office somewhere with a boss lording over me, telling me what to do. I was done with suffocating rules, I knew that for sure. But when I thought about the life I was going to create for myself, I also imagined it to be a lot like Heather's life: steady and secure.

I inhaled the crisp, ocean air and smiled at Heather, feeling grateful and lucky to have her as my friend.

"Yeah. I love the feel of European cities, and the gardens sound amazing," I said, not letting on that I had no idea what I was talking about. "Can't wait to check them out."

WHERE THEY ARE NOW

• • •

January 2014

My dad and Debbie eventually built a multimillion dollar pre-paid telecom company, and then lost everything in the telecom crash of 2000. They have since adopted four children from Russia and my dad, now in his mid-seventies, is back at it again—working to build his next million-dollar business. At the height of his telecom business success, my dad gave my mom a check containing full payment for all the years of child support he owed her.

Three years after divorcing Earl, my mom married James, a Mormon convert from England. He is an amazing, kind, generous man. Together, they served Mormon missions in India, Myanmar, and Indiana.

. . .

Connie lives on five acres of land in Florida surrounded by horses, dogs, and cats. She recently earned her master's degree in information systems.

After graduating from the University of Utah with a degree in communications, I briefly worked at two small newspapers in Utah before moving to Seattle, where I eventually met my husband. I spent years alternating between freelance writing and marketing before embracing my writing dream full-time thanks in large part to our two daughters, who taught me that pursuing my dream is the best example I can set for them.

Heather and I remain close friends.

ACKNOWLEDGMENTS

. . .

I couldn't have told this story without the help of Connie, who has been an incredible friend and supporter throughout all the years I have worked on it. Along with reading and rereading the manuscript, she has spent hours on the phone with me, sharing her memories and thoughts from our childhood, and correcting any inaccuracies she found.

I also couldn't have moved forward with this book if I didn't have the love and full support of my parents. This story covers challenging times and events that I know they would both like to forget. But they understood how important it was for me to tell this story and both stood behind me—which means everything to me.

I owe a special thanks to my husband, John Janeway, who convinced me that *Hippie Boy* was a story worth telling, encouraged me when I got discouraged, and constantly prodded me to dig deeper when he felt the writing wasn't what it could be.

Thanks also to my daughters, Sydney and Hannah, whose belief in me is worth the world.

Hippie Boy wouldn't be where it is today without my agent, Jenny Bent, and my editor at Berkley, Denise Silvestro, who both believed in the book and took a chance on my story. I'm also grateful for the feedback and guidance provided by my initial editor, Erin Brown. I owe a big thanks to Filina Niemeyer, Heather Riley, Nicole Healy, Juli Saeger Russell, Sydney Janeway, Stephanie Hall, Libby Hyland, Andrea Ziegler, Yamilet Reyes, Pam Perry, Casey Kleinman, Mary Moore, Kayla Moore, Lesley Boyd, and Janice Papolos, who all volunteered their time to read early drafts of this manuscript and provided detailed, invaluable feedback. Thanks also to my writer friends Thea Chard, Suzanne Rosenwasser, Stephanie Durden Edwards, and Laura Novak, who have all traveled this journey with me.